Beyond Management

Beyond Management

Ian Lennie

SAGE Publications
London • Thousand Oaks • New Delhi

First published 1999

SAGE Publications Ltd
6 Bonhill Street
London EC2A 4PU

SAGE Publications Inc
2455 Teller Road
Thousand Oaks, California 91320

SAGE Publications India Pvt Ltd
32, M-Block Market
Greater Kailash – I
New Delhi 110 048

British Library Cataloguing in Publication Data

A catalogue record for this book is
available from the British Library

ISBN 0 7619 6257 3
ISBN 0 7619 6258 1 (pbk)

Library of Congress catalog card number 99–072773

Typeset by Keystroke, Jacaranda Lodge, Wolverhampton
Printed in Great Britain by Athanaeum Press, Gateshead

CONTENTS

LIST OF FIGURES

ACKNOWLEDGEMENTS

I would like to acknowledge the assistance and encouragement of Andrew Metcalfe, Steve Linstead, John Hassard, and particularly Anne Game, whose combination of discipline, encouragement and inspiration let me imagine that this work was possible. Also my partner Lesley King who supported, encouraged and advised me, but had the wisdom and patience not to question too closely what was going on. Thanks also to the managers who gave so generously of their time but who, to preserve anonymity, cannot be acknowledged individually. The University of New South Wales Faculty of Arts and Social Sciences also generously assisted with a writing award.

Acknowledgement is also made for the following permissions granted:

To the South Australian Health Commission, South Australian Community Health Association and the Commonwealth Department of Health, Housing, Local Government and Community Services for Figure 1.1 from J. Auer, Y. Repin and M. Roe (1993) *Just Change: The Cost-Conscious Manager's Toolkit*.

To Luzac Oriental for Figures 2.1–2.10 from D. T. Suzuki (1927) *Essays in Zen Buddism*.

To Lucien Stryk for his translation of Ikkuy's poem 'Void in Form' from L. Stryk and T. Ikemoto (ed. and tr.) (1981) *The Penguin Book of Zen Poetry*.

To MacLennan and Petty Ltd for Figure 5.2 from P. Hawe, D. Degling, J. Hall (1990) *Evaluating Health Promotion: A Health Worker's Guide*.

To A.S. Byatt for British Commonwealth and EEC rights to publish extracts from her story 'Art Work' in *The Matisse Stories*. London: Chatto and Windus (1993), and to the Peters Fraser and Dunlop Group Limited on behalf of A.S. Byatt for publication rights for the rest of the world.

INTRODUCTION

Managing is a part of the fabric of everyday life: we manage, or fail to manage, our family, our finances, our career, our exams, our next dinner party. In one way or another managing is something everyone is expected to accomplish. It is a competence of living. Management, however, is a profession, the province of an elite group of people with increasingly specialized training. What is it, then, that we do when we manage, and how does the managing we do in everyday life relate to professional management? These are the questions I shall be exploring in the following pages, questions which will address recognizably conventional management issues, as well as issues of language, organization, and the nature of experience.

I use the term 'managing' for that activity of meaningfully organizing ourselves in daily life, including our daily life in management if we happen to make our living as managers. The term 'management' I use to refer to the professional institution. While this study concentrates on professional managers, it is really their 'managing' – the way they live their lives in the workplace and the way this brings about organization – that will be the focus of my argument.

But if this book is about professional management and everyday experience, it is also about language, and particularly about poetry. This emphasis on poetry may seem surprising, because poetry is largely excluded from the everyday life of contemporary society. Language, however, is inseparable from daily life. Contemporary social and cultural theory would go further and say that experience is textually constituted – that there is nothing outside of text – very convenient philosophy for scholars, a cynic might suggest! But to grasp the full implications of the textuality of our world we need to get beyond the notion that language is a medium through which we somehow refer to a world outside us. And here poetry is important, because poetry is a form of language that works by establishing us as experiencing beings *within* the world. It creates meaning by creating the world in us and us in the world. Understanding how poetry works shows us how language is something that grows from the very fabric of our organization. Poetry, then, reveals to us something about the nature of organization. But organization is what management claims as its province, so management may need to come to terms with poetry if it is to understand its 'core business'.

This book, therefore, will have relevance for students of management and organization studies and for managers who wish to reflect about their practice; but as managing reaches beyond this rather specialized domain and into everyday life and experience, there will be findings of broader interest for social and cultural theory. Perhaps it will also even encourage a few poems, or at least help managers and students discover the poetry that is all around them!

Managing and Management

That managing is an issue for everyone was first impressed on me as a child. I used to overhear my parents talk anxiously about some friend or relative having 'a nervous breakdown'. I was never very clear what this meant, and I had never seen it happen, but it was a common enough event to be a part of everyday conversation. The nearest I could ever get to an explanation was that the person in question 'couldn't manage'. Managing, then, was about being sane, about coping, about not breaking down. It was something everyone was expected to do. Its very ubiquity seemed to preclude definition, except by the shadow implied but not stated in that euphemism, 'nervous breakdown', the shadow of madness and the lunatic asylum. Managing was ordinary enough, but not managing had dire consequences.

How you went about managing, therefore, seemed to be an issue of some importance. My parents were not great readers, but one of the few books they did possess was a handbook on management. Mrs Beeton's *The Book of Household Management* (1861) has probably been the most successful management text ever written. This massive volume (over 1,100 pages) sold more than 60,000 copies in its first year, and by 1868 sales were on the way to 2,000,000 (Spain, 1948). Well into this century it was commonly given as an engagement or a wedding present, and I presume this was how it came to be on my parents' shelves. Its title and its extraordinary popularity suggested that 'management' was something connected to everyday living – to 'managing' in the sense that I have been using it.

For Frederick Taylor, the founder of scientific management, whose work laid the basis for the rise of management as a profession in the twentieth century (Clawson, 1980: 216), management was also about everyday life, but it by no means drew its strength from that. Indeed, he prescribed management as the remedy for 'the great loss which the whole country is suffering through inefficiency through almost all our daily acts' (Taylor, 1911: 7). Everyday life, for him, was mismanaged – a source of inefficiency. Scientific management, on the other hand, had the capacity for national transformation through its ability to take control, not only of industry, but also everyday experience. Near the other end of the century, claims about the importance of professional management are no less sweeping. 'Perhaps there is no more important area of human activity

than managing', state Koontz and O'Donnell (1978: 4) in their intro-
ductory text on the subject, a text which, despite an opening gesture in
that direction, has very little to say about everyday life.

From saving the world to saving us from insanity, there is a common
assumption of importance in these accounts of 'managing' and 'management'. But there is also a gulf between the very claim that management
is a profession and the assumption that it is within the grasp of any
householder, and indeed a basic competence of normal living. Are
'management' and 'managing' connected, or do they arise from quite
different sorts of experience? That question thrust itself on me through
two experiences of my own with professional management, the first as a
trade union organizer and antagonist to management, and the second as
a professional manager myself, whose peers were often also managers.

My active involvement with trade unionism arose from an experience
of management as profoundly disorganizing. This was in the early 1980s
at the beginning of an era of public sector 'reform' that has come to be
characterized as 'managerialism'.[1] I was employed in an Australian State
Health Department at the time that a major restructuring, the first of many
as it turned out, was announced. It abolished the unit I was working in
along with many others, on the basis of a report put together with no
consultation and seemingly having no rationale in the work the Department was supposed to do. It provoked widespread outrage which in turn
led to a protracted industrial dispute, a dispute in which I myself took a
leading role. That dispute required considerable skill in managing, but I
had little practical trade union experience and the union itself had no
experience in widespread and spontaneous rank and file action. What
intrigued me was the way I would seem to know exactly what to do at
pivotal moments without either any desire to control events, or any sense
of what the outcome might be. These events seemed, in a sense, to
organize themselves through my experience of them.[2] I was managing,
but not controlling them. Here then, on the one hand, was a management
that, in my opinion, was not managing, and, on the other, a managing that
was not management.

Management Literature and Training

That capacity to manage in and through experience was something that
continued to intrigue me later as a professional manager. I had obtained a
position as manager of a non-government health organization where
I had been previously working. I began looking around for guidance
both from the formal disciplines of organization and management studies,
and from the literature addressed to managers by the plethora of 'gurus'
with whom the field of professional management abounds.[3] I can make
no claim to have read exhaustively in these fields, but what reading I did
proved a frustrating experience. Certainly I came across some useful

information and techniques, but it was as if all that reflecting on management seemed to come from outside the lived experience of it; it assumed
the manager as a pre-existing entity outside the space of his/her
management and trying to impose on it a culture, vision, objectives, set
of values, or personality. It seemed to me that the activity of managing, of
creating meaningful organization in experience, had been absorbed by
professional management and its agenda of setting experience right.
Management as an institution appeared to have subsumed managing as
an activity.

This corpus of management and organizational writing was not without
its critics. A number of empirical studies had revealed a gap between
what managers were supposed to do and what they actually did (see
especially Hayles, 1986, for a review of this literature) a gap that led Reed
(1989: 170) to conclude 'that current managerial thinking and action is
trapped within an ideological frame of reference that holds an increasingly tenuous relationship to the real world that late twentieth century
managers inhabit'. The logic of Reed's comment might lead one to look for
an 'ideological frame of reference' that related more closely to 'the real
world'. In fact there was a body of literature deriving from neo-Marxism
through critical theory to Foucault that claimed to do just this (e.g.
Braverman, 1974; Offre, 1976; Burrell and Morgan, 1978; Edwards, 1979;
Salaman, 1981; Fry, 1986; Knights and Willmott, 1986; Jackall, 1988; Reed,
1989; Deetz, 1992; Alvesson and Willmott, 1992). While I found much here
that I could sympathize with, there was nothing to indicate how I might
manage better. Critical and Marxist management theory seemed to start
and end in opposition, outside of management, and yet entirely defined
by it. I found it frustrating that none of these writers related their insight
to their own experience of managing: managing of academic departments,
of conferences, of careers, of publications, of identities. In short, critical
theory seemed to depend on and perpetuate the gap between professional
management and managing as a competence of living presumably
possessed by all these authors.

If the literature on management and organization proved to be frustrating, the plethora of management training courses available seemed
equally so. This frustration was not only mine. Of all the managers I
interviewed in the course of writing this book, only one had found formal
management training of much use beyond the opportunity it afforded for
general reflection and networking with other managers. The following
comment may be taken as typical:

> Once I'd started I no longer felt I had the time to be sitting for days. I didn't
> think those courses were useful anyway. I felt I could learn this stuff better
> by practising it. It was a lot of textbook kind of stuff.[4]

This lack of relevant training was apparently not just an artifact of the
particular sector in which I worked. The following quotation from the UK

Graduate Admissions Council is highlighted in the Report of the Australian Government's Industry Task Force on Leadership and Management Skills (Karpin Report, 1995: 154):

> The curricula of business schools have recently concentrated much more on the building of elegant, abstract models that seek to unify the world economic system than on the development of frameworks to help students understand the messy, concrete reality of international business.

It seems that in management training, as well as in management studies, criticism was rife about a gap between what professional management was supposed to do, and the way managers experienced management.[5] Is the solution, then, as the UK Graduate Admissions Council seems to suggest, to develop 'frameworks' that can be better aligned to 'messy, concrete reality'? The problem with this formulation, as with changing our 'ideological frame of reference', is that it already locates the manager *outside* the reality he or she is managing or studying, aligned more or less badly with it according to the framework used. I, on the other hand, felt I was *in* that reality, not somehow outside and needing to be aligned with it. My interest therefore was drawn not so much to different frameworks as to different ways of investigating reality.

Experience and Embodiment

It became evident that the problem that I was experiencing was not just limited to the study of management and organization. The self-representation of management as in some important sense outside the reality it was managing had its roots in traditions of power and knowledge dating back at least to the Renaissance, traditions that separated the subject from the object of knowledge and control (Foucault, 1970). At that time it seemed to me that these issues were being challenged more constructively in other disciplines. In sociology, the influence of deconstruction, with its emphasis on the radical textuality of the world, had led Game (1991) to challenge that discipline's claim to provide knowledge of society as an extra-textual reality, with the aim of changing or reforming that reality in the future. The parallels seemed obvious between, on the one hand, traditional sociology and, on the other hand, professional management's project of gaining knowledge of an external reality in order to control and change it. The postmodern understanding of the world as textual questions that very separation of knowledge from an external reality which it would know and seek to control. If there is no knowledge outside of text, there is no privileged point from which to know or control it. While such an approach, applied to management, raises the question of management's very relevance – how can you manage what you cannot control? – it also offers the possibility of thinking management differently. Game's sociological concern with 'the immediate, the lived of everyday life and experience, and with transformations in the now' (ibid.: ix) accorded with my interest in relating professional management to the managing of lived experience, and to my sense as manager of being in the space of my managing rather than outside it.

A concern with lived experience is, inevitably, a concern with embodiment, because bodies are the locus of our experience of the world. Sociology, however, as Bryan Turner pointed out in *The Body and Society* (1984: 30) 'has little to say about the most obvious fact of human existence, namely that human beings have, and to some extent are, bodies'. He attributes this absence partly to sociologists' desire to distance their discipline from social Darwinism and, more recently, sociobiology. Yet the absence of bodies has meant a devaluing in sociology of experience arising from embodiment, and an impoverishment of understanding of our participation in nature and the material world generally.[6]

The 'body' of social Darwinism and sociobiology is not an experiencing body, but a system of evolving responses and adaptations. One intellectual tradition that has struggled to re-unite the body with its experience, phenomenology, offers a sense of embodiment that challenges this separation. Merleau-Ponty in particular, in his concept of 'flesh', strives to conceptualize a double nature of bodies that is, at the same time, not a dualism. On the one hand, my body participates in the world of bodies and is one object amongst others. On the other, my experience of this participation marks it out from all other bodies as the unique locus of my being in the world. My experience is uniquely mine, but it comes from my embodied participation in what is beyond me (Merleau-Ponty, 1968). It is this double nature of bodies that makes 'the body' central to a sociology that is concerned with immediate, lived experience rather than the investigation of safely distanced factual objects.[7] But as the body is also the locus of experience of managing, an understanding of managing could profitably begin here.

The Writing of Embodiment

Merleau-Ponty has been criticized from a Buddhist philosophical tradition for trying to restore the body and its lived experience through a language of theoretical abstraction (Varela et al., 1991). One does not need to appeal to Buddhism, however, to find a non-abstract body of writing that deals directly with lived experience: this can be found to hand in literature. Management guru Tom Peters (1992: 375), in fact, explicitly contrasts the richness and complexity of life as it appears in literature and is experienced in private life, with the impoverishment of writing and thinking about management and organization:

The richness of life, which we accept as private selves and when we turn to novels or poetry, seems abandoned at the front door of the business or public agency establishment.

Literature is of interest for managing not just because it *reflects* the complexity of an experience, but because it is a way of *organizing* experience without losing that complexity. Literature, when it works successfully, organizes in embodied reality, not in abstraction prior to, or outside that reality. As D.H. Lawrence (1961: 110) wrote:

> The novel is the highest example of subtle inter-relatedness that man has discovered . . . If you try to nail anything down, either it kills the novel, or the novel gets up and walks away with the nail.

Not surprisingly, people involved in thinking about literature were discussing issues of embodiment long before 'the body' became a feature of contemporary cultural theory. Here is Lawrence again, writing in the 1920s (1961: 103): 'Oh, yes, my body, me alive, *knows*, and knows intensely.' The body for him was the locus of knowledge. Disembodied experience, on the other hand, was the source of much of the psychopathology being then identified through psychoanalysis (Lawrence, 1960). The novel, as a truly embodied form of organization, offered the possibility for more unified, re-embodied experience. For T.S. Eliot, writing in 1927, a capacity for poetry was a capacity for organization in experience, experience that came not just from the heart, but from the whole body, 'the cerebral cortex, the nervous system, and the digestive tract' (Eliot, 1963: 290). In 1937 F.R. Leavis, in distinguishing literary criticism from philosophy, wrote of the 'fuller-bodied response' (Leavis, 1963: 213) that reading poetry demands: Such a habit of reading, he claimed, developed 'a growing stability of organization' that related the relative values of poetic experience without resort to 'a theoretical system or a system determined by abstract considerations' (ibid.: 213). This tradition of literary thinking is one that values embodied experience as a source of organization, as opposed to organization as a 'nailing down' of experience by abstractions and pre-conceived plans.

Metaphor and Postmodernity

Literature has often been distinguished from other forms of writing by its 'fictional' character. Unlike scientific or philosophical writing it is not supposed to be a transparent medium through which reality is revealed. In particular, its reliance on metaphor and figurative language in general, has led it to be regarded as unreliable, if not downright misleading, as a source of knowledge (Ricoeur, 1977). Recently, however, there has been

renewed interest outside of literary studies in metaphor, and figurative or
troped language in general, an interest that coincides with postmodern
questioning of any pre-existing reality that guarantees the status of a real
or proper meaning. Derrida (1976; 1982) explicitly links a radical claim
for metaphor with this questioning of the real in his assertion that the
nature of experience is textual. Because metaphor, for Derrida, is the form
of textuality itself, there is no knowledge that is not metaphorical. But
metaphor, the very essence of poetry, is the language of embodiment. It
organizes through the body. Thinking about and experiencing metaphor
thus offers a way of connecting textuality, embodied experience, and
organization, and this is why it will be central to my exploration of
managing in experience.

Metaphor has in fact been the subject of some discussion in management and organization theory in recent years, a debate stimulated largely
by Gareth Morgan's *Images of Organization* (1986). Morgan investigated
the metaphoric basis of different concepts of organization (as machine,
brain, organism, political struggle, etc.) and the way these shaped the
sort of questions people asked. Groundbreaking as this study has been, it
is still limited to an observer/framework/reality model of experience,
with different metaphors operating as different frameworks, like looking
at organization through different sets of spectacles. But a framework
model itself begs the question of how that framework is lived. In my
investigation, then, I have not so much followed Morgan in searching out
particular metaphors of organization and management, as looked at metaphoricity itself as an organizing principle in the managing of experience.
Metaphor allows us to relate otherwise disparate experiences through our
bodies.

Morgan's interest in metaphor and imagery was an indication that
management and organization studies could not long be immune to the
dislocations of postmodernity. At the time of writing, postmodernist
issues have in fact proliferated, albeit at the fringes of these disciplines
(e.g. Clegg, 1990; 1992; Reed and Hughes, 1992; Hassard and Parker, 1993;
Boje et al., 1996; as well as numerous articles and discussion in journals
like *Organization Studies* and the *Journal of Organizational Change Management*, the latter devoting an entire issue (5 (1), 1992) to the topic). Outside
the academy, management guru Tom Peters has increasingly embraced
postmodernity, perhaps at the cost of his mainstream status, with *Thriving
on Chaos* (1987) and especially *Liberation Management* (1992).

The debate on postmodernity and organization generally divides into
two parts: 'postmodernism as either a historical periodization or a
theoretical position' (Hassard, 1996: 59). On the one hand, is there a postmodern organizational reality (or post-organizational reality), and, if so,
what is it like? On the other hand, is there a postmodern way of thinking
(or, really, of being) that reveals the whole project of management and
organization to be an untenable modernist fantasy? (Parker, 1992). Some
of this discussion will be taken up in the following chapters, but, as with

the critical management literature discussed earlier, I find very little of it addressed to the lived experience of managers. One exception is Peters (1992), who embraces both sides of the debate – ie that there are post-modern organizations and that they are effectively unmanageable – and explores the experience of managing in these situations. His contribution will be addressed in Chapter 8.

Experiences of Managing

Clegg (1990: 15), commenting on what he saw as the beginnings of a 'wholesale importation' of postmodern thinking into organization studies, called for the need to connect this movement 'not only with debates of a similar conviction but also with the discourse of everyday sites of life'. In developing this book I have focussed primarily on professional manage-ment, but with an interest in how the managing that happens there relates to everyday life. In doing this I have taken up Clegg's suggestion quite literally. The experience I draw on is, first, my own as manager of a non-government community health organization. During this time I took extensive notes reflecting on my own practice. Managers spend a lot of time talking to other managers, and this gave me the opportunity to interview around fifty managers of community health services, other non-government agencies and a few academic departments, all of whom I dealt with in the course of my work and who were, in a sense, my colleagues. These interviews followed a semi-structured format that was basically designed to get managers talking about managing as they experienced it: when it started and finished for them, its pleasure and pain, and what they saw as important and interesting. The format varied to follow particular issues the interviewees brought up, or my current interest or worry. Managers proved an easy group to interview, being educated, articulate, and interested in reflecting on their work. No-one whom I approached refused to be interviewed.

In seeking out interviews I was not interested in accumulating a statistically valid profile of managers in the sector where I worked. I simply interviewed until I had sufficient accounts of the experience of managing to be worth writing about. In this I kept in mind the observation of Durkheim (1965: 114–15) that 'it is neither necessary nor always useful to heap up numerous experiences upon each other; it is much more important to have a few that are well studied and really significant'. Nevertheless, some characteristics of this group should be mentioned as bearing on their experiences, and I include myself in this general characterization. All the managers had been at least 12 months in their current job. All were in charge of relatively autonomous work units, ranging from separate organizations with their own boards of manage-ment, to largely independent units within larger organizations, including a few university departments; so none were within a traditional bureaucratic structure, and all had considerable managerial autonomy. None of these organizations were managed for profit, and most had some overt concern for social justice. The organizations were not large employers: they ranged from, at the smallest five, to around 100 staff, with a median of 25. Number of staff, however, was not necessarily an indication of range of responsibility, as these organizations often operated within networks of relatively independent agencies, professionals, and volunteers. Staff employed were predominantly professional, although with a sizeable administrative and maintenance group. All managers except four had some training in another profession prior to getting into management. As management is a very male-dominated profession (Kanter, 1977; Hearn, Sheppard et al., 1989; Collinson and Hearn, 1996), I tried to interview an equal number of men and women.

My interviews with these managers and my own notes provided a collection of written texts, to which should be added, as well as the reading I have already mentioned, a considerable body of industry literature on management, organization and related issues, much of which came across my desk in the course of my work. It is these texts that form the basis of the following study. This is not to imply the limitation of a supposed reality that the text only reflects, but can never entirely account for; it rather means that the written text, which is just one manifestation of textuality, requires a certain discipline to realize it as experience, and it is 'in the rigour of the analysis which proceeds out from the text that the value of (the) analysis lies' (Linstead, 1993: 69). There is an implied limitation, in the absence of other texts that might have contributed to the value and richness of the result. In particular, these are very much managers' accounts of their experience, and staff accounts of being managed by these managers would undoubtedly have added another dimension to the story. Also of interest might have been the managers' reactions to what I made of their accounts, reactions which I was only able to incorporate in a couple of cases.

Textuality proliferates infinitely, and so, as part of the intertextual process, does analysis; at a certain point, however, you decide that there is something worth writing about, a decision that enforces limits and, therefore, a certain turning away from what is beyond those limits. At the same time, however, those very limits provide a bearing within the infinite sea of possibility that is the textuality of the world, and so open it up to us and us to it. This complementary process of closure and opening is no more than the frustration and the hope of managing, as I hope to show in the following chapters.

A Map of the Terrain

Some readers like to have a map of what is coming. The following outline, necessarily rather abstract, caters for them. Others may prefer to go straight to Chapter 1.

Chapter 1 Management without Body. Modern professional management presents itself as outside its own experience, observing it, and using it to know and control a world which it is assumed to reflect. But, because we experience the world by being embodied in it, to be outside our experience is, paradoxically, to be embodied outside our own body and outside the body of the world. Management, then, often appears doubly divided: from itself, and from the world that it manages. This division has its roots in post-Renaissance philosophical and scientific traditions that separate a perceiving subject from an object of perception, this separation being a strategy for establishing objective knowledge or truth. This subject/object division conceals a desire for power: to know but not be known, to perceive but to remain inviolable as subject, to control bodies including one's own but not to be embodied. This desire is realized practically through the conjunction of the scientific tradition of knowledge with technologies of control to produce the possibility of a world that can be remade according to a pre-conceived vision, or world view. Frederick Taylor founded his theory and practice of management on the separation of the management of work from the process and experience of doing it, a separation that replicates the separation of subject and object. This separation, where management as mind is placed outside, and controls, the body of work, laid the foundations for modern professional management. The achievement of this management is constantly produced outside of itself, leaving the self disembodied – empty. This emptiness must then be obsessively filled by new projects of control. Management, paradoxically, becomes extremely productive, but its productivity is never enough.

Chapter 2 Nothing to Manage, The Ten Cow-Herding Pictures. A traditional Zen guide to spiritual awareness; shows how a different philosophical tradition takes the distinction between subject and object to be illusory, and shows how abolishing this distinction seems to abolish the necessity for management. This insight that subject and object were never separated in the first place offers a starting point for thinking about managing practices that are less disembodying.

Chapter 3 Managing Management. The constant demand management creates for yet more management leaves its practitioners constantly grappling with the unmanageability of their own task. Many of them experience management as actually or potentially invasive of their sense of self, simultaneously overwhelming and emptying. Being able to manage management effectively seems to require access to a space of embodiment outside of management, a space where the self becomes re-embodied. This access actually works best when it is available within management itself, that is, when the management space is not singular. Successful managers have, within the space of their professional activity, experiential access to the unmanaged. They move between managing and not managing, and relate the two experiences in their bodies. The relational quality of experience proves to be, significantly, metaphoric in character. Understanding how metaphor works allows us to bring contemporary theories of textuality to the process of managing within experience.

Chapter 4 Managing and Poetry. There has been a lot of writing about metaphor in recent management and organization theory, but it always fails to go far enough. Metaphor relates language, organization, and our embodied experience. It does this by enacting the relational organization of the outside world within our bodies. This enables us to experience the possibilities of connection between things. A metaphoric capacity is thus a capacity for organization. Poets develop this capacity through language; a good manager develops it through organization of themselves, other people, and the material world. Like poetry, managing requires an openness to experience that is defeated by the sort of disembodiment explored in Chapter 1. This openness allows organization to happen from within a situation, rather than being imposed from outside or on top of it. It is the situation that organizes, not the manager as organizing subject, although the manager is part of that situation.

Chapter 5 Managing and Order. Management requires an openness to experience to allow the possibilities for organization to develop within a situation; however, it also requires closure, where the multiplicity of experience is focussed on a single outcome. This is the most recognizable moment of management, and its epitome is planning. But managers are characteristically ambivalent about planning, and an understanding of metaphor allows us to see why. The singularity and closure implied in planning seems to be the reverse of metaphoric, but an analysis of how managers work with lists, plans and structures of ordering shows us that closure only works if it too works metaphorically – that is, if it embodies the self as organized within the multiplicity beyond it. Otherwise the order produced by planning may be experienced as disorganizing. This metaphoric understanding of managing helps us to understand how formal procedures are both helpful and unhelpful.

Chapter 6 Managing and Disorder. Clearing away disorder has always been seen to be an essential part of management, yet this clearing activity also provokes ambivalence because of the threat of pollution through proximity to disorder. This ambivalence stems from attempting a non-metaphoric relation to disorder. It is particularly evident in the housekeeping function of management and in the position of those who perform it: secretaries, cleaners, etc. Clearing away, or cleaning, is a process of making a whole and integral self, a process that seems, in its separation of order from rubbish, the reverse of metaphoric. However, using Mary Douglas' formulation of disorder as symbolic of creative formlessness shows that the separation of order and disorder only works if it acts metaphorically: that is, if it creates us as clean and ordered in relation to the formless possibility of disorder. We can see how this happens, and fails to happen, in some essential but seldom discussed areas of management: domestic management, office management and in the actual disposal of waste and rubbish.

Chapter 7 Managing and Art. A.S. Byatt's (1993) story, *Art Work* offers a remarkable example of successful managing that flows neither from the purity of order, nor from immersion in disorder, but from a metaphoric relation between the two.

Chapter 8 Managing Beyond Management. To manage we must exceed the order we have created. The embodied character of metaphor means that exceeding our own order requires an embodiment that also exceeds itself. Our body is a becoming, not a being. Through managing we are taken up in a movement beyond ourselves. The work of Tom Peters intimates this movement. However it is better understood through Terence Turner's concept of the play of tropes, an account of managing as a flow of meaning that relates an embodied self to the outside world in which that self moves, a flow that is demonstrated through experiences of managing well. Through managing we live relationally, and it is the quality of those relations that determines how well we have managed. This applies as equally to professional management as to managing in everyday life.

Conclusion: Letting Go. Professional management and managing in everyday life are closely related, but they are not the same. The metaphorical movement that links us to what is beyond ourselves can move us out of professional management; but this movement, in itself, is also a form of managing. To be successful, closure must be metaphoric. Just as new beginnings cannot be entirely empty, so endings cannot be entirely empty either. For an ending to be experienced, something must continue beyond it, and that continuity must be made from what has been left behind. Endings and beginnings are related by managing.

Notes

1 'Managerialism' has become a critical term for an increasingly influential involvement of professional management in public sector activities during the 1980s, with an agenda of greater efficiency brought about by methods derived from private sector experience (see Yeatman, 1987; 1990; Pollitt, 1993; Rees and Rodley, 1996).

2 As an example: my sense that the dispute had become unwinnable came to me quite suddenly and certainly, not as the result of calculation or discussion. I had been attending a hearing at the New South Wales Industrial Commission, and as my colleagues were cheerfully discussing the next move I ceased to hear or be one of them. I felt a profound gloom, as if enveloped in a cloud, and with it the conviction that we could not win, and that we had to get out of the situation as quickly and with as little loss as possible. I knew I had to manage a way out of the

confidence and euphoria that I had been involved in creating. I seemed to recognize a pivotal point in that dispute through my immersion in the situation. It was this recognition that allowed me to act confidently and decisively.

3 Kerfoot and Knights (1996) relate the constant rise of gurus in management to the insecurity inherent in the management enterprise. Managers sense that the expertise on which their legitimacy is based does not have the certainty and stability of scientific knowledge, and so are constantly searching for new and plausible solutions.

4 Excerpts are from managers interviewed as part of this study. These interviews will be discussed in more detail later in the Introduction.

5 The advice of management gurus and consultants is apparently held in no higher regard if a recent story by Deirdre Macken in the *Sydney Morning Herald*'s magazine *Good Weekend* (April 5, 1997: 46) is anything to go by. She writes:

> By last year management consultancy in the US was worth $US25.9 billion and the book sales were $US930.4 million, despite 70 per cent of managers saying management tools don't deliver and four out of five failing to finish the books.

6 It could be countered that management has specifically addressed the issue of the body through the discipline of ergonomics, which seeks to understand and control the relationship between work situations and the bodies that occupy them. This body, however, is not the living, experiencing body, but the body as an object of study, as Murrell (1965: xiii) makes clear when he defines ergonomics as 'the *scientific* study of the relationship between man and his working environment' (my emphasis), an environment which, incidentally, for him, excludes 'man's relations with his fellow workers, his supervisors, his management and his family' (xiii). The same objectification is evident in the systems approach taken by Zinchenko and Munipov (1989: 13), for whom '[E]rgonomics studies the systems regularities of man–machine–environment relationships in the process of work or during preparatory operations'.

7 Cf. Merleau-Ponty (1964: 163): 'Visible and mobile, my body is a thing among things; it is caught in the fabric of the world, and its cohesion is that of a thing. But because it moves and sees, it holds things in a circle around itself. Things are an annex or prolongation of itself; they are incrusted into its flesh, they are part of its full definition; the world is made of the same stuff as the body.'

1

MANAGEMENT WITHOUT BODY

Towards the end of his study of the production of space, Henri Lefebvre makes a sweeping proposition:

> The whole of (social) space proceeds from the body, even though it so metamorphoses the body that it may forget it altogether – even though it may separate itself so radically from the body as to kill it. The genesis of a far-away order can be accounted for only on the basis of the order that is nearest to us – namely, the order of the body. (Lefebvre, 1991: 405)

This proposition, calling for a radical reassessment of the basis of order, implies an equally radical reassessment of the way that we manage. The space we actually inhabit, Lefebvre asserts, is not the empty space of geometry, but an order. This order is not us, but it comes from our experience of ourselves: it comes from our body. The body and the order it produces are always in relation: but sometimes that relation, Lefebvre suggests, is paradoxical, denying its own basis. Order becomes disembodied and so does the body to which it relates. In management, this paradoxical relation – this withdrawal from an embodied order, and so from one's own body – is so often the norm that it ceases to evoke surprise or even comment. Here, as shown in Figure 1.1, is an example from the cover of a recent manual, *Just Change: The Cost-Conscious Manager's Toolkit* (Auer, Repin, and Roe, 1993).

A disembodied head – or, rather, several heads overlapping like the pages of a book – tilts forward from a base, as if hinged. A handle projects from the scalp. Within the head is a stylized eye, and a row of arrows seems to project the eye's gaze outward. As well as the eye, a curious collection of objects floats within the space of the head: a screw, a globe, a key, a nut and washer, a running figure, a book, and three question marks. This limbless and trunkless head, as fantastical as a Salvador Dali dream, is the very image of disembodiment. Yet in its place on the cover of a current management text, it can be taken for granted, as no more than a skilful illustration of its theme. How does this come to be an acceptable representation of management, evoking identification from managers rather than, say, repulsion, fear, or incomprehension? And what sort of order might proceed from a management imagined in this way?

Figure 1.1 *Cover Illustration:* The Cost-Conscious Manager's Toolkit
(Auer, Repin, and Roe, 1993)

The Mind's Eye

We accept this image, of course, because it is embedded in intellectual and practical traditions going back at least as far as the Renaissance – traditions that themselves give rise to our current conceptions of management. This particular image is interesting because it lets us decipher in some detail, if only we can get past its taken-for-grantedness, how these traditions shape our thinking. The image depends on what we shall call, for the sake of brevity, a Cartesian conception of knowledge. A mind, or subject, conventionally located inside the head, is separated from the outside body of the objective world, and from its own body. But this separation begins from the body, as Descartes himself makes clear. Seeking for models of practice that might establish secure knowledge, he singled out those craftsmen around him who, 'fixing their eyes on a single point, acquire through practice the ability to make perfect distinctions between things, however minute and delicate' (Descartes, 1985: 33). In his appeal to craftsmen Descartes is not prefiguring William Morris. The eye is the most distancing of senses, and in the embodied and plural eyes of these craftsmen Descartes finds a figure for the single mind's eye of the philosopher, which alone distinguishes truth:

> We must concentrate our mind's eye totally upon the most insignificant and easiest of matters, and dwell on them long enough to acquire the habit of intuiting the truth distinctly and clearly. (ibid.: 33)

Like the Cartesian philosopher, the subject in our illustration looks outward, as indicated by the line of arrows, not from the eyes of the body, but from the single eye of the mind. Through observation, the eye brings back knowledge, as indicated by the book, the globe, and those symbols of inquiry, the three question marks. Through this eye the subject looks out to the 'far-away', in Lefebvre's term, but is not in or of it.[1] In effect, the knowing subject, or observer, has no embodied identity, embodiment being a characteristic of the objective and observable world. This disembodiment of the subject is expressed in Descartes' famous proposition 'Cogito, ergo sum – I think, therefore I am', where identity is equated with pure thought. The eye, observing from a distance, becomes a metaphor of this disembodied relationship between observer and observed. Management, as we shall see, is born out of this subject/object relationship.

The Contaminating Body

This transformation of the observer from embodied subjectivity to pure thought creates a powerful conception of knowledge, because it allows the possibility of an objective world uncontaminated by the status or location of the observing subject, a subject which is not body for the purposes of knowledge. The same knowledge is potentially available to anyone who follows the same rules of observation. Moreover, as anyone's observation is open to the scrutiny of anyone else, observations can be challenged and corroborated. Observations from any number of subjects can also be accumulated, as they are all consistent, so a possibility of a cumulative understanding of the world is opened. As well as advantages, however, this conception of knowledge creates some difficulties. The relationship of the body to knowledge is made problematic: the body becomes only a possible source of contamination. Even the eye becomes the mind's eye. A knowledge that begins in experience – observation – paradoxically becomes increasingly distrustful of any particular experience. The more secure knowledge becomes, the more it is both everybody's and nobody's. Emotion contaminates objectivity by embodying the subject, thus shifting it from its securely objective position into the world under scrutiny. Emotion, then, in this Cartesian framework, should have no part in the quality of knowledge itself.

While management is not philosophy, nor indeed science, the scientific outlook to which Cartesian philosophy has given rise has a critical role in structuring a contemporary understanding of management. Both management and science are deeply implicated in an epistemology that divides the disembodied subject from the object of knowledge, and that regards the embodied, feeling subject as crossing this divide and polluting objectivity. Here are some examples from managers I interviewed. The first shows a commonly expressed distrust of subjectivity. This manager carefully distinguishes between the 'I' that is her subjective self, and the knowledge on which she bases management decisions:

> I undertook to gather the information. Most of it is information that can't be disputed, therefore there's been no conflict in accepting that. If I'd just come in and said 'I believe aboriginal health is an issue here and we've got to do something about it', I'd get nowhere. But by being able to go about it in a methodical way, gather information . . . it's been accepted.

Objective knowledge 'can't be disputed'. While an 'I' gathered the information, that information is not contaminated by subjectivity; it is not a product of 'I believe'; it is gathered 'in a methodical way'. Being independent of subjectivity and therefore of emotion, its acceptance involves 'no conflict'. As knowledge exists outside subjectivity there is, in a sense, no-one to disagree. A shared belief in objective knowledge is thus an important means of gaining agreement. Indeed, Frederick Taylor claimed that if management could be put on a scientific basis it would mean 'for the employees and the management who adopt it . . . the elimination of almost all causes for dispute and disagreement between them' (Taylor, 1911: 142).

The contaminating role of emotion is expressed by a second manager when expressing concern that she is too closely engaged with her workplace:

- Do you think of it as a family?
  Yes, unfortunately.
- Why 'unfortunately'?
  Well, one should be much more objective than that.

Here a feeling of engagement or closeness to what is being managed shifts the manager away from detachment, and so undermines objectivity. Objective knowledge comes from being withdrawn into the mind's eye: disengaged from the objects of knowledge and from oneself, insofar as one is involved with those objects.

The Big Picture

The further the seeing eye withdraws, the larger the perspective, the greater the scope of the objective world that falls within its vision and the further removed the disembodied subject from a reciprocal relationship with that world. The fantasy that is implicated in the desire to be 'a viewpoint and nothing more' – the mind's eye in effect – is wonderfully conveyed by De Certeau's (1988: 92) evocation of New York from the summit of the World Trade Centre:

To be lifted to the summit of the World Trade Centre is to be lifted out of the city's grasp. One's body is no longer clasped by the streets that turn and return it according to an anonymous law; nor is it possessed, whether as player or played, by the rumble of so many differences and by the nervousness of New York traffic. When one goes up there, he leaves behind the mass that carries off and mixes up in itself any identity of authors or spectators. An Icarus flying above these waters, he can ignore the devices of Daedalus in mobile and endless labyrinths far below. His elevation turns him into a voyeur. It puts him at a distance. It transforms the bewitching world by which one was 'possessed' into a text that lies before one's eyes. It allows one to read it, to be a solar Eye, looking down like a god. The exaltation of a scopic and gnostic drive: the fiction of knowledge is related to this lust to be a viewpoint and nothing more.

The 'objectivity' of the all-seeing eye is not an indifference to the world. It is implicated in a fantasy of power. This fantasy is not apparent in the knowledge itself, yet it is a condition of its production. This implication of power in the production of knowledge links the project of science directly to management. The idea that the manager is someone who can see more than other people and whose power flows from this larger perspective is suggested in the very term for a common managerial activity, 'to supervise'. To super*vise* is to over*see*.[2] It marks the manager's position as special and apart:

I like my role as a person who can aspire, or look at things differently. The supervision role.

This apartness allows the manager, unlike others, to be 'a big-picture person' who can see across all the components of a system:

> I think . . . the fundamental thing, I'm a big-picture person and I like being at a level where I can actually see across a system. And I think that's the thing I like most about it [managing], that I know what's actually happening in different areas, and I also get the external picture of what's happening across as well.

Another manager also expresses this 'lust to be a viewpoint' as one of the pleasures of managing:

> Having the overall perspective. I enjoy seeing all the moves about to happen, and the possibilities of moves.

In contrast, this manager, who does not see herself as a 'big picture person' worries that this is a failing:

> I'm very comfortable. Sometimes that worries me. I think I'm too close to the grass roots of the service.

The 'grass roots' is perspective degree zero, at the opposite pole to the top of the World Trade Centre. Feeling that she ought to be nearer the latter pole, more distant and detached, makes being 'very comfortable' uncomfortable. It 'worries' her. Comfortable is not powerful; it is not apart.

Another suggestive image of loss of overall perspective appears in this manager's criticism of the level of management 'above' him. (Significantly, management is often described in ascending and descending 'levels' implying greater or lesser imagined perspective and distance from the 'grass roots'.):

> The other problems are at the Department level . . . the lack of vision as it runs around like a headless chook that doesn't have a plan or a vision that either exists or is in a way complementary to what we are doing.

If effective management can be imagined as a seeing eye in a disembodied head, as in our opening illustration, ineffective management is its opposite, a headless body. A headless body can have no perspective, and its fallible body is all too visible as it 'runs about'.

The complaint that the 'headless chook . . . doesn't have a plan or a vision' extends the visual metaphor of knowledge from space to time. Just as the all-seeing eye takes in the larger perspective of what is around it, it also 'sees' the future as part of that perspective. This larger perspective on time also sets managers apart:

> I might be thinking one, two years ahead, where people I deal with at an operational level might be thinking about next week.

Sometimes you've got this whole picture of where you want the organization to be in five years, but you know that if you actually sat there and told everybody what your strategy was and let them all in on it, at this point in time they wouldn't understand it or necessarily believe in it, and you know that you've got to let them, at the time that it's right, into bits of the strategy that you've got or the vision that you've got.

This capacity for superior vision distinguishes the manager, who is just 'muddling', from the true leader:

And that's interesting too, making a distinction between managing and leading. At [my health centre] there's been a push that we [managers] are leaders, and, in fact, what we end up doing a lot of the time is managing, and I think they're very different words. I think about managing along in the same way as you think about muddling along. Whereas leading is about having an ideal and going towards it and getting people along with you.

This manager speaks about an 'ideal' rather than a 'vision', alerting us to the fact that managerial vision is not a matter of clairvoyance, of actually seeing into the future, but a projection of an experienced present that is visible now as an *idea* to the mind's eye. Such a vision implies a shift in the role of the inward eye from a Cartesian receptor of the truth of the objective world to the site where the shape of that world is imagined. 'This lust to be a viewpoint and nothing more' (De Certeau, 1988: 92) implicates the Cartesian view of the world in a fantasy of power, but withdrawal to a position of an all-seeing eye does not confer power in itself. The shift from knowledge to vision invites the alignment of the outside world with the picture in the mind's eye. But how is that fantasy realized? How can we change the outside from the inside?

From Vision to Handling

Abrams (1953), in his study of metaphors of creation in Europe from the Renaissance to the nineteenth century, traces a shift from the mind as a reflector holding a mirror up to nature, to a projector that lights nature with the lamp of the mind's own inward light. Such a shift from a predominantly passive to an active meaning of vision suggests an increase in confidence that the subject of the subject/object distinction can not only observe and understand, but actively intervene in the outside world, bringing that world's future into line with an imagined or ideal present. Foucault, in his work on medicine (1973) , and on forms of discipline in Europe in the seventeenth, eighteenth, and nineteenth centuries (1991) charts how this confidence comes about. The shift from observation to investigation also starts from the body, but not from the eye. Foucault reveals, on the one hand, a world scrutinized, watched, and surveyed by the mind's eye, a world that is studied and documented scientifically; at the same time however, he charts the parallel development of an array of practical methods for handling, control, and regulation. He describes these developments as two 'registers': of Cartesian scrutiny, on the one hand, and of techniques of discipline and control, on the other. The registers develop separately, yet together:

> The great book of Man-the Machine was written simultaneously on two registers: the anatomico-metaphysical register, of which Descartes wrote the first pages and which the physicians and philosophers continued, and the technico-political register, which was constituted by a whole set of regulations and by empirical and calculated methods relating to the army, the school and the hospital, for controlling or correcting the operations of the body. These two registers are quite distinct, since it was a question, on the one hand, of submission and use and, on the other, of functioning and explanation: there was a useful body and an intelligible body. (Foucault, 1991: 136)

The intelligible body is known through the mind's eye; the useful body however, has not so much been observed as moved, assembled, shaped, and disciplined. The useful body is one that can be manipulated, *handled*. It is significant, then, that the word 'manage' first comes into English in the context of *hand*ling, in this case of horses:

> The word **manage** seems to have come into English directly from *maneggiare*, It[alian] – to handle and especially to handle or train horses. Its earliest English uses were in this context. The f[orerunner] w[ord] is *mandiare*, v[ulgar] L[atin] – to handle, from r[oot] w[ord] *manus*, L[atin] – hand. **Manage** was quickly extended to operations of war, and from e[arly] C16 to a general sense of taking control, taking charge, directing. (Williams, 1983: 190)

Management first arises not so much from a privileging of sight as of an active touch, of *hand*ling. Techniques of handling create the connection that makes the intelligible body conform to the vision of the inner eye. The possibilities implied by the mapping on to each other of Foucault's two 'registers' are succinctly stated by Karl Marx (1958: 405) in his eleventh thesis on Feuerbach:

> The philosophers have only *interpreted* the world in various ways: the point, however, is to *change* it.

Knowledge has been supplanted by control as the meaningful relationship of the subject to the outside world. Ironically enough, Marx's thesis has become not only the slogan of revolutionaries, but also of contemporary management, as this manager makes clear:

> Certainly I think a lot of my motivation is to change, to make an impact on the system and to see it to some degree be different after I've come in contact with it.

This ability to systematically change the world is what, for Friedrich Engels (1958: 89), distinguishes man from the animals: 'the animal merely *uses* external nature', while 'man by his changes makes nature serve his ends, *masters* it'. This mastery is the realization of that desire for power that is only implicit in the gaze of the inward eye, but is completed in techniques of the hand.

For Engels, the visionary eye is itself the product of the hand. Man as animal evolves firstly to *homo faber* – the maker – and it is *homo faber* who creates *homo sapiens* – the knower.[3] For Engels, the key moment in the evolution of humanity was the moment when man first stood upright so that 'the hand became free' (ibid.: 81). This freedom of the hand allowed manipulation of the environment in a way that in turn developed the brain, and this development eventually led to the extension of the hand through the making of tools. Tools multiply the effect of the hand. But through the multiplication of labour made possible by tools, the mind can separate itself from its own labour, and thus from its own hands:

[T]he mind that planned the labour ... was able to have the labour that had been planned carried out by hands other than its own. (Engels 1958: 87)

Or, as one manager put it:

I want to get things done and I never have enough time, but now there's forty or sixty of me. The staff are like an extension of me.

This separation of the mind that directs labour from the hands that carry it out not only multiplies the body, but leads to a further qualitative development, a stage that puts the multiplied body at the disposal of a premeditated vision. As Engels (1958: 88) puts it, '[t]he further removed men are from animals, however, the more their effect on nature assumes the character of premeditated, planned action directed towards definite ends known in advance'. Man, he argues, is at this stage in a position to re-create nature, and hence himself. The external world, including humanity itself, has become manageable, at least in theory – a space waiting to be aligned with the vision of a mind that has become separate from it.

The importance and persistence of tool imagery in management should now be apparent. Tools shift the emphasis from *knowledge* of the objective world to *change, manipulation* and *control*. Hence, in our opening illustration, they mingle – in the form of a screw, a key and a nut – with the symbols of knowledge. This mingling of symbols inside the head suggests, moreover, that knowledge too has become a tool, of value to the mind insofar as it contributes to changing the world. Not only knowledge, but the body itself is subsidiary to a mind that, according to Engels, the body itself originally created. It is particularly apt, then, that our toolkit illustration depicts a complete body only *within* the toolkit/hand. The body depicted, moreover, is not a real body, but a puppet or manikin.

The body, as body, is just another tool at the service of a mind that knows
through mastery.

Management as Science

If Engels formulated the possibility, through a unity of science and
technology, of shaping the world to a premeditated vision, and in so doing
shaping humanity itself, it was Frederick Taylor, not the revolutionaries,
who systematically set about realizing the possibility. Taylor's continuing
importance arises not so much from his particular methods of control over
work processes (for a comprehensive critique of these see Braverman,
1974), but from his presentation of an ideal type (Weber, 1949) of
management as the establishing of control over an external environment
from a position of disembodiment. In him we see at their clearest the
development and consequences of this position.

A second reason for an interest in Taylor is his concern not just with
a system of ideas as such, but with their actual implementation. In fact
it was through implementation, he argued, that knowledge was to be
derived. In all areas of scientific management 'practice has preceded
theory, not succeeded it', he claimed in an address to the Cleveland
Advertising Club (quoted in Copley, 1969: I, 348). He disagreed when
Edwin F. Guy, the first Dean of the Harvard Graduate School of Business
Administration, wanted to design his management courses around
Taylorist principles, arguing that training should be based in the factory,
not in the university (Clawson, 1980: 207). In his systematic emphasis on
the primacy of implementation, Taylor is exemplary of that movement
from science to manipulation whose background I have briefly traced.
Because of that, his own career reveals better than most the sort of
embodiment from which this approach proceeds.

Taylor's gravestone is marked 'Father of Scientific Management',
a phrase used as sub-title of his first extensive biography, written in
the 1920s by Frank Barkley Copley (1969), an avid enthusiast of Taylor's
methods. The way Copley describes Taylor's first involvement with
industry is a good illustration of that relation between eye, hand and mind
implicit in the union of science with technologies of discipline. Brought up
amongst the Philadelphia Quaker elite, Taylor expected to do law at
Harvard, and embarked on a course of study at a college in Exeter, New
Hampshire, preparing himself for advanced academic training. However
the intensity of the study program damaged his eyesight to an extent that,
at the end of two years, he felt that he could not continue an academic life.
With the eye ruled out as the predominant organ of learning, he now felt
obliged to work with his hands. These terms are Copley's, who goes on to
remark of Taylor that 'as boy and man, all his forces centred in his head',
adding, significantly, that he 'hated to do things with his hands' (ibid.: I,
76). Nevertheless, hating it as he did, in 1874 he became an apprentice

pattern-maker and machinist at the Midvale Steel Company in Philadelphia, a shop owned by friends of his family. It was here that he persuaded his employer in 1881 to allow him to conduct a series of time-study experiments that developed into the project of scientific management.

Copley describes the Midvale works that Taylor entered as not just a space of manual work, but one to a considerable degree controlled by the 'hands'. In places like Midvale, workers did not own their workplace, decide their working hours, or what it was they produced; nevertheless, they had considerable control over the way a job was done and the time it took to do it. In other words, they managed much of their own work. Management, and what they were engaged in producing, were not separate activities. A single workman or group of workmen would order the materials, design the job, and complete a complex task from beginning to end. Workmen would have their own tools and be responsible for their maintenance. Job skills would be passed on orally and by practical demonstration. The managing of work was very much bound up in the experience of it.[4]

Separating the Head from the Hands

Taylor, frustrated at management's lack of control over the pace and method of work under this system, set about scientifically establishing a 'fair day's work'. His method was to decisively separate management from the experience of work, taking control from the 'hands' (the workers who did the work) and putting it in the 'head' (the management who planned and controlled it). This procedure created the basis for professional management, 'something which up to that point had only a protean existence' (Clawson, 1980: 216). This setting apart of a managing function modelled the Cartesian separation of mind and body. The body of work – the workers themselves, their materials and movements – was set up in the manner of an object before Taylor's scrutinizing gaze.

Taylor undertook at Midvale an immense project of observing and measuring everything about the work processes there, documenting every separable motion in each particular task and meticulously timing it. His instructions for doing this work of observation follow Descartes' injunction to make 'perfect distinctions between things, however minute and delicate':

(a) Divide the work of a man performing any job into simple elementary movements.
(b) Pick out all useless movements and discard them.
(c) Study, one after another, just how each of several skilled workmen makes each elementary movement, and with the aid of a stop watch select the quickest and best method of making each elementary movement known in the trade.

(d) Describe, record, and index each elementary movement, with its proper time, so that it can be quickly found (quoted in Copley, 1969: I, 227).
(e) Study and record the percentage which must be added to the actual working time of a good workman to cover unavoidable delays, interruptions, and minor accidents, etc.
(f) Study and record the percentage which must be added to cover the newness of a good workman to a job, the first few times that he does it.
(g) Study and record the percentage of time that must be allowed for rest, and the intervals at which the rest must be taken, in order to offset physical fatigue (quoted in Copley, 1969: I, 227).

Work is reduced to elementary observable motions. Any more complex elements – those that might connect the workman to an embodied subject – are included only as annoying inefficiencies: 'newness', 'minor accidents', 'physical fatigue'. As we have seen, in the production of scientific knowledge, the involvement of embodied subjects can only be considered a liability.

From these elementary particles a proper or objective way of doing the job can be constructed through a process of selection and addition:

(h) Add together into various groups such combinations of elementary movements as are frequently used in the same sequence in the trade, and record and index these groups so that they can be readily found.
(i) From these several records, it is comparatively easy to select the proper series of motions which should be used by a workman in making any particular article, and by summing the times of these movements, and adding proper percentage allowances, to find the proper time for doing almost any class of work. (quoted in Copley, 1969: I, 227–8)

Taylor applied exactly the same method to developing new machinery. Kakar (1970) gives this account of his development of a revolutionary steam hammer that kept its alignment through the elasticity of its parts:

First he devoted two years to collecting from all over the world exhaustive data on hammers until he was able to isolate those instances in which some of the parts of each of the various hammering machines had never broken. He then copied the design of each of these, collecting one element from one machine, another from another, another from a third (Kakar, 1970: 113)

Taylor's method, which he presents as a method of science, is at the same time a method of discipline. It not only produces knowledge in a certain way, but sets up the outside world to make it conform with the results of that knowledge. It combines a system of observation with a system of manipulation. The separation of workers as objects of surveillance, the analysis of their activity into elementary particles of movement, the assembly and timing of a required set of movements, and the prescription that, in future, every worker conforms to those movements and times, all these steps are a replication of the techniques of discipline that Foucault documents as developing in the army, prisons, and educational institutions as a '"physics" or an "anatomy" of power' (Foucault, 1991: 215). The intelligible body requires a useful body. Thus the very process of scientific investigation re-creates the workplace as a space of discipline where management exercises power over every detail of the work process.

So the frustrated intellectual who hated to do things with his hands set up a scientific system of management that both separated him from manual work and allowed him to control it. Copley (1969: I, 350) sums it up thus:

> The genius of the system that Taylor built may be summed up in this: that from a centre corresponding to the brain of an animal organism, it provides for intensive control, 'according to clearly-defined scientific rules and formulae', of all the methods, implements, materials, and general conditions of work, and in consequence the volume, flow and quality of work.

Appropriately a whole new division of the workplace, the planning department, is set up to reflect this control of head over body:

> The practical use of scientific data also calls for a room in which to keep the books, records etc. and a desk for the planner to work at. Thus all of the planning which under the old system was done by the workman, as a result of his personal experience, must of necessity under the new system be done by the management in accordance with the laws of science. (Taylor, 1911: 38)

This planning department according to Braverman (1974: 125) spawns a new version of production because 'the process of production is replicated in paper form, [creating] a variety of new occupations, the hallmark of which is that they are found not in the flow of things but in the flow of paper'. Braverman's tone is somewhat dismissive of what he refers to as this 'shadow form of production' (ibid.: 125). In fact, the paper form is not just production 'replicated'; it actually anticipates production, so that any actual moment of production is merely an example of its planned form. We can see this legacy at work in the current concern for quality management. The International Standard (ISO 9000 series) for quality systems, for example, requires that 'all the elements, requirements and provisions adopted by an organization for its quality system should be documented in a systematic, orderly and understandable manner in the form of policies and procedures' (AS\NZS ISO 9004.1: 5). Because these documented policies and procedures enable 'continuous control . . . over all activities affecting quality' (ibid.: 40), they in turn must be controlled, through a document control system, as closely as the processes they control.[5]

The Body Protests

'Every technique', Merleau-Ponty observed, 'is a "technique of the body".
A technique outlines and amplifies the metaphysical structure of our
flesh' (1964: 168). It is instructive, then, to look at what we are told of
Taylor's relationship to his own body. Kakar here describes his approach
to play:

> Fred was severe in his observance of each and every rule of the game. In a game
> of croquet he would carefully work out the angles of the various strokes, the
> force of impact, the advantages and disadvantages of the understroke,
> overstroke, and so on, before he started to play. In cross-country walks he
> constantly experimented with his legs in an endeavour to discover the step
> which would cover the greatest distance with the least expenditure of energy.
> (Kakar, 1970: 18)

In play and in work, his body was an instrument to be used with
maximum efficiency. However it did not always co-operate. From a very
early age Taylor was apparently subject to insomnia and nightmares.
At a time when Freud was exploring the unconscious through dreams,
Taylor's approach to the same phenomenon is here described by a
childhood friend, Birge Harrison:

> Being of an observing nature, he soon noticed that when he awoke from one of
> these obsessions he was invariably lying on his back – and from this he argued
> that there must be some connection from the position in which he lay and the
> distressing mental disturbance. Thereupon he constructed for himself a sort of
> harness of straps and wooden points, the latter so arranged that whenever in his
> sleep he turned over on his back the points in question would press the dorsal
> muscle and at once awaken him. I think it was the Spartan nature of the
> contrivance that impressed me at the time, and for that matter still impresses
> me. (Copley, 1969: I, 58)

As described here, his body is not a source of understanding about
himself, but an object to be observed and disciplined. Taylor's sense of
embodiment is such as to make him relate to his body as something outside himself. But he is not, of course, literally disembodied, so his denied
body seems to return in its own way to haunt his mind like a fleshly ghost.
Taylor eventually discarded his harness, but he was never cured of his
nightmares, and could only sleep in a bolt-upright sitting position,
propped up by pillows (Copley 1969: I,58). Copley comments:

> There is evidence that, haunting some part of the nature of this courageous
> man, was the ghost of a fear, a horror. (ibid.: I, 59)

Taylor's body also had its own say about his obsession with the proper
time for every movement. In a remarkable example of the psychopathology of everyday life, the man who was synonymous with time study

was, apparently, 'notoriously unpunctual for his personal appointments, which he often "forgot" due to his "poor memory"' (Kakar, 1970: 22). While the body may have been forgotten in the process of creating of order, it did not go away, but asserted its presence by imposing a forgetting of the very order that its absence created. The order that proceeds from the forgotten body, this suggests, will always be a troubled order.

If Taylor's own body made its protest about scientific management, the corporate body protested as well. The emptiness of working in a system that excluded all personal engagement from the work itself led to constant labour protest. Taylor's disciples, Lilian and Frank Gilbreth (Spriegel and Myers, 1953: 105) pose the question bluntly:

Does not the monotony of the highly specialized subdivision of work cause men to become insane?

The answer, they claim, is 'No', because specialization itself produces further knowledge, and even if it does not, the worker has other options. He can 'join the planning department' or 'become a teacher of other men'. If all else fails:

He can plan the spending of the extra money that will be in his pay envelope on the next pay day, and can consider the intellectual stimulus that the extra pay will purchase. (ibid.: 106)

To persuade workers to stay on the famous Model-T Ford production line, set up on Taylorist principles, Henry Ford had to pay twice the current average wage – the famous five dollar day (Littler, 1982). The greater productivity of scientific management made higher wages possible, and so a trade-off developed: emptiness at work, what Gouldner (1969) tellingly referred to as 'the unemployed self', for the possibility of a fuller life outside it.

But protest did not only come from labour; indeed, Taylor claimed that he had considerably more trouble from management. The reason was not just the labour troubles and disruption caused by the introduction of production lines. Managers could also see that the system introduced to give them complete control could, paradoxically, undermine that control. Taylor was dismissed from Bethlehem Steel where he was attempting to install his system, running into concerted opposition from middle management, board members and the President of the company Robert P. Linderman. On Linderman's attitude Copley (1969: II, 145) records 'the words of a gentleman who is still connected with the company':

Mr Linderman thought Mr Taylor was employed to introduce piece work and help us in general to increase our production; but what Mr Taylor did was to go into the works and start a revolution.

Ironically, the man who claimed that introducing the rule of science would lead to 'the substitution of peace for war; the substitution of heartily brotherly cooperation for contention and strife,' (Taylor, 1911: 30) had to retire from hands-on management because of the level of strife involved. After the unsuccessful struggle at Bethlehem he wrote:

> The nervous strain of this work can hardly be appreciated by one who has not actually undertaken it, as it involves one squabble after another, day in and day out. (quoted in Copley 1969: II,167)

Filling the Empty Body

Towards the end of his life, and subject to increasing depression, Taylor made a revealing admission:

> Every minute of my day here is filled up now, and yet somehow I don't seem to accomplish much of anything. (quoted in Kakar, 1970: 186)

The 'filled up' day is experienced as empty. But if, following Lefebvre, we think of the space of that day as the space of an order proceeding from the body, the emptiness of that space is the correlate of the emptiness of that body – a body that is imagined as outside itself. The space of the day itself is not just given, but produced through an experience of disembodiment. The desire to experience that space as full is a desire to be re-embodied. Hence the incessant activity. Emptiness is filled by an obsessive activity of controlling the body of the world (including, in Taylor's case, his own body). This controlling activity, then, because it is a constant subduing of bodies against their resistance, is experienced as struggle. Struggle becomes the guarantee of embodiment. It is the paradoxical experience of embodying oneself against the order of the body – of living through resistance. 'Character' was Taylor's term for this self, experienced through struggle.[6] In a lecture entitled 'Success' (quoted in Copley, 1969: I, 84) he wrote:

> *Character* is the ability to control yourself . . . the ability above all to do things which are disagreeable, which you do not like. It takes but little character to do difficult things if you like them. It takes a lot of character to do things which are tiresome, monotonous, and unpleasant.

Insofar as Taylor's struggle succeeds, he fills the emptiness of time/ space with the results of his struggle. But as these results are embodied outside of him, this fullness is no sooner effected than it is experienced as empty. Once the outside is under control, struggle ceases. In order to restore a sense of embodiment, the emptiness must then be filled with more struggle, a frantically productive, but finally futile process of trying to reembody oneself through a process of disembodiment. It is when the struggle ceases that the futility becomes apparent, so it cannot ever afford to cease.

Management Unmanaged

Taylor's project is announced as one of control, but the unending struggle to fill an emptiness that he is in fact creating, suggests that it is the project that is controlling him. It was this capacity of the project of mastery to turn on itself, which Martin Heidegger was to explore in 'The Question Concerning Technology'. Technology, for Heidegger, was not so much a way of getting things done as a way of being human – a way which created 'the realm of human capability as a domain given over to measuring and executing, for the purpose of gaining mastery over that which is as a whole' (Heidegger, 1977: 132). He describes the generalization of technology in a way that recalls the early military derivations of the concept of management, as the creation of a 'standing-reserve':

Everywhere everything is ordered to stand by, to be immediately at hand, indeed to stand there just so that it may be on call for a further ordering. Whatever is ordered about in this way has its own standing. We call it the standing-reserve (*Bestand*). (ibid.: 17)

Heidegger describes how the river Rhine has been thus created as standing-reserve by a hydroelectric plant:

In the context of the interlocking processes pertaining to the orderly disposition of electrical energy, even the Rhine itself appears as something at our command. The hydroelectric plant is not built into the Rhine River as was the old wooden bridge that joined bank with bank for hundreds of years. Rather the river is dammed up into the power plant. What the river is now, namely a water power supplier, derives from out of the essence of the power station. (ibid.: 16)

Meaning is created, not through Cartesian observation, but through handling, manipulation, management. 'Unlocking, transforming, storing, distributing and switching about are ways of revealing' (ibid.: 16). The Rhine has not merely been put to use, it has been revealed as something different: it is a resource. Power and knowledge have thus become entwined. In Foucault's later formulation, 'far from preventing knowledge, power produces it' (Foucault, 1980a: 59). But whose power are we referring to? If the Rhine is now revealed as a resource by the process of control, why not the controllers themselves? The Rhine appears to be at our command, but it is the process of damming up that elicits that command. The systematic control of resources becomes itself controlling. If everywhere, everything is ordered to stand by, then, Heidegger asks, 'does not man himself belong even more originally than nature within the standing-reserve?' (1977: 18):

when man, investigating, observing, ensnares nature as an area of his own conceiving, he has already been claimed by a way of revealing that challenges him to approach nature as an object of research, until even the object disappears into the objectlessness of the standing-reserve. (ibid.: 18)

The 'standing-reserve' becomes like Taylor's empty day, a sort of limbo or waiting room for a future that always recedes into further ordering – a truly vertiginous prospect:

[If] man in the midst of objectlessness is nothing but the orderer of the standing-reserve, then he comes to the brink of a precipitous fall; that is, he comes to the point where he himself will have to be taken as standing-reserve. (ibid.: 18)

The picture of the manager standing by as a tool for the process he is managing is perhaps the revolution that so alarmed the President of Bethlehem Steel. The final irony is that the controlling mind itself is simply another product of the process of control. This irony is actually present in our toolkit/head illustration, where the disembodied controlling mind is itself a toolkit whose handle waits to be grasped by a manager who is also a toolkit, and so on in a series of receding images, with no final subject–manager to pick up the handle. The manager has himself become standing-reserve, on call for further ordering along with the rest of the manageable world. The dream of a management which, powerful and untouchable, shapes the world according to its own ideas, becomes something of a nightmare.[7] The very distinction on which its security rests, the separation of subject and object, mind and body, dissolves into an endless standing-by for further standing-by.

Our opening illustration, then, depicts a conception of management which, when its logic is pursued, is ultimately unmanageable. Such a management creates an order, but one that alienates itself from its own embodied experience, resulting in an obsessive need for further ordering. Its desire for mastery ensnares the would-be master in an endless round of projects of control inserted in a process that is itself out of control.

Notes

1 I am not arguing here for some sort of physiological determinism. Vision does not have to be experienced in this disembodied way. Merleau-Ponty (1964: 164), for example, offers a quite different relation between the body and vision:

Since things and my body are made of the same stuff, vision must somehow take place in them; their manifest visibility must be repeated in the body by a secret visibility. 'Nature is on the inside', says Cézanne. Quality, light, color, depth, which are there before us, are there only because they awaken an echo in our body and because the body welcomes them.

2 Cf. Foucault's (1991: 200) description of supervision in Bentham's Panopticon:

Each individual in his place is securely confined to a cell from which he is seen from the front by a supervisor . . . He is seen, but he does not see: he is the object of information, never a subject in communication.

3 For an account of the modern revival of Engels' *homo faber*, see Metcalfe, 1995: 107ff.

4 There is some argument as to whether United States' industry at this time was predominantly based on craft production or internal contracting (Clawson, 1980; Littler, 1982). Clawson presents Taylor as 'the Napoleon of the war against craft production' (1980 202), whereas Littler argues that craft production had already been undermined by the less benign relations of internal contracting, in which the level of control exercised by ordinary workers was considerably more limited. Even under the latter system, however, the major drawback from the capitalists' point of view 'was that some organizational processes were, literally, out of their control' (Clegg, 1990: 90).

5 Ironically enough there is evidence that managers generally prefer verbal to written communication (Mintzberg, 1973) to the extent that Gowler and Legge claim 'that management may be viewed essentially as an oral tradition' (1983: 197). That managers in practice feel constrained by their own systems of management explains why 'paper' loomed as a problem for most of the managers I interviewed. Any process of control represents a limitation on the fantasy of absolute freedom to manage, a fantasy of being above or outside the world under control. As one manager complained:

Paper means you have to do something. It makes demands. You have to respond.

6 Taylor's indefatigability in finding opportunities for struggle is even evident in his relations with his cat, Putmut. Copley relates that, on moving to semi-retirement at his country residence, Boxley, Taylor had an entire hill removed from behind the house in order to reveal the view. Putmut would not go outside while the men were digging. Copley (1969: II, 230) describes Taylor's response:

What! Day after day with no outdoor exercise! that would never do. So Taylor attached a cord to the cat's collar, and proceeded to drag him out. It was all done – systematically. Each day Putmut was dragged a bit further, until finally dragger and draggee got away down to (the gardener's) lodge.

7 This is a nightmare Merleau-Ponty (1964: 160) shares with Heidegger:

If this kind of thinking (thinking operationally) were to extend its reign to man and history; if, pretending to ignore what we know of them through our own situations, it were to set out to construct man and history on the basis of a few abstract indices . . . then, since man really becomes the *manipulandum* he takes himself to be, we enter into a cultural regimen where there is neither truth nor falsity concerning man and history, into a sleep, or a nightmare, from which there is no awakening.

2

NOTHING TO MANAGE

The Ten Cow-Herding Pictures (Suzuki, 1927), as shown in Figures 2.1–2.10, are a traditional text of Zen Buddhism, showing ten stages on the path to enlightenment, told as a story of a man searching for, and finding, his lost cow. Approaching this search, by way of the previous chapter, as a management problem, provides an illuminating counterpoint to a more traditional reading. If Taylor reached an impasse where the distinction between subject and object dissolved into a nothingness that encompassed both, the Zen text takes this impasse as a moment of enlightenment, and proceeds beyond it. My interest is in how this opens up possibilities for managing beyond the disembodied presentation I have been discussing so far. (My abbreviated version of the more traditional reading is given in italics and my managerial reading in normal print.)

Looking for the Cow (Figure 2.1) *A man stands alone in a landscape looking bewildered and holding a tethering rope. He has lost his cow. But the cow is himself, so she has never gone astray. Rather, he has been led astray by the deluding senses, wandering further and further from home.*
A man perceives the outside world as out of control. His cow is missing. He needs the cow for his livelihood; he must find her and restore the order that sustains him.

Seeing the Traces of the Cow (Figure 2.2) *By studying the Sutras the man begins to understand; he has found traces of a way. He begins to see that the objective world is only a reflection of the self, but he is still confused as to truth and falsehood.*
The man scrutinizes the outside world for information, which he finds. Cow prints show him a direction.

Seeing the Cow (Figure 2.3) *With his senses in harmonious order the man can now begin to experience the cow as nothing other than himself. With proper seeing there is no room to hide.*
His information was correct, as indicated by the cow's behind coming into view. Seeing the cow, however, is one thing, but having her at hand is another. She must now be managed and brought under control.

Figure 2.1 *'Looking for the Cow' from* The Ten Cow-Herding Pictures *(Figures 2.1 to 2.10: Suzuki, 1927)*

Figure 2.2 *'Seeing the Traces of the Cow'*

Figure 2.3 *'Seeing the Cow'*

Catching the Cow (Figure 2.4) *He has taken hold of the cow, but after being long in the wilderness she is wild and unruly. He needs all his discipline to keep her in subjection.*
The man lays hands on the cow, but she is still wild and out of control. A struggle ensues. He needs the tools of discipline, the whip and the rope, to manage her.

Herding the Cow (Figure 2.5) *The cow now follows the man as one thought follows another. But thoughts may stray and he must not be separated from the whip and the tether.*
The cow has now been managed and will follow the man home, but only with constant surveillance and intervention. Management has been successful, but there is still a need to maintain the achievement. Control requires constant struggle.

Coming Home on the Cow's Back (Figure 2.6) *The struggle is over. The man is no more concerned with gain or loss. He plays his flute, in harmony with everything. His eyes are no longer fixed on the earth.*
The struggle is over and the outside world has been brought under control. The cow is so manageable she can be put to use as a form of transport. She will even find her own way back, crossing the bridge without direction. The man can devote himself to his hobby of flute-playing, not even looking where the cow is going.

Figure 2.4 *'Catching the Cow'*

Figure 2.5 *'Herding the Cow'*

Figure 2.6 *'Coming Home on the Cow's Back'*

The Cow Forgotten, Leaving the Man Alone (Figure 2.7) *The man is home. There is no need for the cow, she was only symbolic. The whip and rope are no longer needed. He sits quietly dreaming.*
With the cow looking after herself, and the outside world completely under control, the man can retire, but he cannot sleep. As dawn breaks on another day without struggle, he is awake, wondering, anxious. Perhaps the cow has strayed again and he should start to look for her.

The Cow and the Man Both Gone Out of Sight (Figure 2.8) *All confusion and division are set aside, and serenity alone prevails; even the idea of holiness is no longer relevant. There is no self, only the vastness of heaven.*
Without another situation to manage there is only emptiness. Either this is death, or a new problem must be found to fill the emptiness and, through the experience of further struggle, reassure the man of his significance.

At this moment our managerial reading of the cow-herding pictures either ceases, because with death there is nothing to manage and no-one to do the managing, or begins again, with a new cow to be found and brought under control.

The Zen version of the story, however, has two more stages.

Figure 2.7 *'The Cow Forgotten, Leaving the Man Alone'*

Figure 2.8 *'The Cow and the Man Both Gone Out of Sight'*

Returning to the Origin, Back to the Source (Figure 2.9) *This title is something of an irony. There is no duality, no inside or outside. Emptiness is fullness. Nature can return and the growth and decay of things with form can be watched, while abiding in the serenity of non-assertion. Everything is the same, and there was no loss or defilement in the first place. The distinction of subject and object was only an illusion.*

Figure 2.9 'Returning to the Origin, Back to the Source'

Entering the City with Bliss-Bestowing Hands (Figure 2.10) *Grown old and fat, the man enters the marketplace, mixing with wine drinkers and butchers. He is not a god with miraculous powers, and he does not stay apart from ordinary people. He smiles broadly, and with nothing to gain or lose, following no footsteps and having no home, he allows everyone to become Buddha.*

Each of these readings begins with a duality to be overcome through discipline and struggle. But the purpose of discipline and struggle for management is to bring the objective world under control while remaining apart from it. In the Zen reading, the purpose of struggle is to bring about the realization that there was no duality to begin with and so no reason to struggle. Both readings arrive at a cessation of struggle. For management this cessation brings an emptiness that in turn provokes anxiety to begin again, so the self will not be experienced as lacking. In the

Figure 2.10 *'Entering the City with Bliss-Bestowing Hands'*

Zen reading there is also a cessation of struggle, which also brings an emptiness, but this emptiness reveals 'that from the very beginning there has never been any real *lack*, because there has never been any self-existing self apart from the world' (Loy, 1992: 153,4). Once the self simply is the flow of experience, as in Figure 2.10, the outside is the inside and the picture is full, although empty of inside and outside. Free of the struggle with duality, one simply lives, as in the last picture.

The two readings also have different implications for embodiment and the order that flows from it. In the management reading the body – the cow – is part of the outside that must be brought under control. But once controlled it is gone again, because the very process of ordering it establishes it as separate to the disembodied self that controls it. The body is only present in the struggle to overcome it. In the Zen reading the struggle is to realize that the body never was separate, and neither was the rest of the world. Once struggle ceases, the body is present because everything is present – but not present *to* anything. The loss of the controlling mind regains the body, while the assertion of the mind always loses it.

What these last two pictures suggest is that, with no inside or outside, there is no need to manage, and the only effective managing is to arrive at that point. But, paradoxically, it is just at that point that managing starts, because it is not the manager that manages the flow of experience, but the flow of experience that manages. What *The Ten Cow-Herding Pictures* suggest is the possibility of managing through experience rather than against it, so restoring the body and the outside world to that headless manager of our opening illustration. Such a managing starts through realizing that the manager and the outside world, including the body, were never separated in the first place – *'the cow is himself, so she has never gone astray'*.

3

MANAGING MANAGEMENT

Managers are not always chronically depressed or overcome with a sense of meaninglessness. If the project of management in its ideal form is inherently unmanageable, how do managers actually live with that in practice? Because that unmanageability of management is bound up with disembodiment, we might expect that strategies for managing will involve ways of remembering and restoring the body – of realizing that, like the cow, it has never gone astray. In this chapter we shall examine the strategies – some successful, some not so successful – of a number of managers, and see what can be concluded from their experience.[1]

Total Management

Taylor's commitment to management was total. It occupied all his available time. It made his workplace, his and his children's education, his garden, his golf, even his relations with his cat, into an occasion for management. But if management was all-consuming, it also 'used up' the manager himself, as his friend Klyce remarks in a letter following one of Taylor's numerous nervous breakdowns:

> He has used up his nervous system to such an extent that he is not permitted to work but half a day. (quoted in Copley, 1969: II, 434)

Unable to manage his own management, Taylor himself had to be managed. 'He is not permitted to work.' His physician now delineated the time in which he lived and how he filled it.

Heedless of this warning, contemporary accounts of management seem to suggest, not just that all life be brought under the control of management, but that there is no life apart from it. Here is James S. Lawson, Head of the School of Health Services Management, University of New South Wales:

> Being a successful manager is certainly not a 9 to 5 job. Success requires commitment 24 hours per day. The 'normal' office hours need to be spent

encouraging and consulting colleagues, participating in meetings, conducting field visits, reviewing, receiving reports and negotiating with other organizations. At the end of other people's ordinary days, is the time to undertake written work, reading and telephoning peers who are also too busy during the day. (1992: 107)

The management day is here distinguished from 'other people's ordinary days' by an absence of division. Management happens '24 hours per day', and if this seems somewhat of an exaggeration, recall Taylor's efforts to manage even his sleep. Moreover, not only is there no time free of management, but no action in that time is insignificant for management. Elsewhere Lawson remarks, a propos of a study showing the manager's day constantly being interrupted by apparently superficial encounters, that 'it can be argued that the successful senior manager rarely has a non-meaningful interaction with anybody else, even those not associated with the organization' (ibid.: 77). Management is all pervasive and charged with meaning even in its most trivial moments. The very sense of busy-ness and the scarcity of time for it all confirm the manager's importance and difference.

Enterprising Nation, a national Report on leadership and management skills tabled in the Australian Federal Parliament in 1995, suggests that the 24-hour a day manager is not a temporary phenomenon. Examining '(t)he Emerging Senior Manager Profile', the Report divides management into three periods. In the 1970s 'The Autocrat' experienced '(s)table environ-ment, relatively low stress' and was 'home to see the kids most nights'. Today, 'The Communicator' experiences a '[t]urbulent environment. High stress, long hours, fears burnout'. By 2010 'The Leader/Enabler' emerges, with '(e)nvironment typified by rapid change, limited term appointment, high pressure, results driven' (Karpin Report: xi). 'Home to see the kids' vanishes with 'The Communicator'; the only hope for the 'Leader/Enabler' to even engender any would seem to lie in the spaces between one 'limited term appointment' and the next!

Not all managers are impressed by this prospect of total management. For this manager it indicated a failure to manage:

> When your first waking thought is work, that usually means there's something pressing you're not managing.

Another manager, one of *Enterprising Nation*'s 'communicators' who does not get to spend much time with the kids, agreed. When I asked her what she liked about management, she replied:

> Very little . . . What I don't like is overload. In the management situation I'm in, there is no way out. It's just full on all the time. Being full on means that my energy levels are entirely spent on work and there's very little time for my family. And that's the necessity of getting the day-to-day stuff. And the frustration for me: I want to be a more strategic manager, and yet the day-to-day stuff is all-encompassing and huge.

Her time is experienced as a space[2] in which she feels trapped, where there is 'no way out'. This space is at the same time full and empty: 'full on' and yet 'all-encompassing and huge'. It leaves her diminished, with her 'energy levels . . . entirely spent' – a disembodied feeling. The space that comes from the body, in Lefebvre's formulation, is also killing it. Being trapped in this all-encompassing space excludes her from two other spaces: her family, and somewhere she could get a perspective on 'the day-to-day stuff' and be a 'more strategic manager'.

What is particularly frustrating for her is that she is in management in order to preserve her family:

> At the moment, to be very honest with you, the only thing that's keeping me in the job is that I'm the wage earner for my family. If I could change that tomorrow I wouldn't be in the job.

However, the family is itself invaded by management. I asked her if she took work home:

> Yep. Of necessity.
> – Do you find that intrusive?
> 'Absolutely, and my family does also.
> – Do you think about work at home?
> Yes, over particularly bad strips. And that's the stress level, not a particularly conscious effort to think about it because I want to.
> – How do you control it?
> I've talked to the General Manager [her boss] about it. I try to do physical activity like sport or walking when time permits. I try to do things with the kids, but I can do less of that than I used to. [long silence]

A number of times she makes reference to being trapped by *necessity*. She says she would leave work 'if I could change that', but she is the wage earner, so she cannot. She talks of 'the *necessity* of getting the day-to-day stuff', taking work home 'of *necessity*', thinking about work because of stress levels, not because 'I want to'. Necessity excludes any sense of a self outside of management. It is, in Heidegger's terms, discovery that you yourself are part of the 'standing reserve': that you are managed, not managing.

Here is another manager who does not feel so trapped, but admits to being 'very driven'. He is driven, among other things, to use a management technique – his diary – to ensure he has access to a time he calls 'sacred':

> [Showing me his diary] I put everything into it. I book sleep, routine travel. That was a funeral I had to go to.
> – In a sense you manage your whole life, not just the office.
> Definitely. If I didn't I'd just end up doing nothing but work. I balance work and the rest of my life. I might work late. I have a rule that if I don't finish I don't take work home. I might plan to work at home till 7.00. Then I finish.

– I see you've planned 7–8 for dinner, and then you go to sleep at 9.30, but there's a blank up till then.

Oh, that's just spare time for anything I want to do. Watch telly etc. I very much integrate my whole life into the book, because, as I said, I'd end up working constantly. I have to actually plan to take time out or it just gets eaten up. I've got stuff booked for me. It's sacred, it's absolutely sacred.

The diary is a technique for allocating time as space, something we will be returning to in Chapter 5. Establishing separate spaces creates boundaries, whereas a single space would end up being filled by 'nothing but work', with his own time 'just eaten up', something that was happening to our previous manager. However there is an interesting slippage of boundaries when he says 'I have a rule that if I don't finish I don't take work home', then immediately follows this by 'I might plan to work at home till 7.00. Then I finish'. The boundaries are not as sure as he claims.

Integrating his life into a book gives him a sense of existing outside something that otherwise might overwhelm him. There is something visibly over that is larger than the 'day-to-day', and is not 'eaten up' by it.[3] It is significant that part of his 'sacred' time is actually blank. It escapes the world of necessity, becoming time for 'anything I want to do'. In so doing it becomes a time when he is recreated or replenished. This blankness recalls the empty moment in *The Ten Cow-Herding Pictures*. This is an emptiness that can become fullness. It is the realm of possibility. By being blank, anything becomes possible, and the future is not contained in the present.

The diary technique, however, seems double-edged. Integrating everything into the book can be seen as trying to contain the uncontainable; a space that is supposed to escape the boundaries of management becomes itself the object of management. As in the quote from Lawson (1992) above, management becomes a 24 hour business, including even sleep. (Was it surprising to learn that this manager had developed an ulcer at the age of 35, sometime after this interview?)

Here is another manager who also confesses to being 'driven'. She also asserts the importance of establishing separate times:

I like to come home and spend time in the kitchen. And certainly when I'm riding, I definitely, definitely don't think about anything to do with this [managing]. That's quite separate . . . Even if I'm absolutely fucked on Friday night I'll get to bed in time to get up, because that's a way of absolutely marking an end of it. Saturday is a day of restoring myself: the ride, doing my washing, filling the house with food, cleaning it. By the end of it, Saturday afternoon, I'll sit down with a glass of wine and think about my own work. (She is an academic who manages her department.)

– So you don't think of managing as your own work?

No. I have to keep it quite separate from what I think of as mine, even if I'm writing about all those things. Isn't that funny? I feel like it's taken over my life. I have to make boundaries and keep it separate, or it just invades. I can't sleep. I can't do other things. It's had a dramatic effect on my friendships. In

some ways I feel, oddly, better about myself since doing this job. The extent
to which I won't let it defeat me. I keep the show on the road.

This manager also keeps times for herself separate from the time of
management. These separate times are not marked in a diary, but they are
marked by days – 'Saturday is a day of restoring myself'. They are about
cleaning, filling, restoring, exercising the depleted body. Like our first
manager, she feels strongly that management time is not hers, and that it
is invasive of what is hers. In fact it has already invaded sleep and
friendship. While she insists that there is a time that is hers, it is the
insistence itself that is most noticeable. When riding she 'definitely,
definitely' does not think about 'anything' to do with management. Even
if 'absolutely fucked' she will get up on Saturday because it 'absolutely'
marks the end of the management week. She has to keep management
'quite separate' from what she thinks of as hers. But interestingly, it is in
this very struggle that she feels good about herself. Thus it is ambiguous,
when she says 'I keep the show on the road', whether she refers to her
workplace or herself. Like Frederick Taylor, it is in the *struggle* to manage
that she experiences herself, and this includes the struggle to manage
management. She might be building a separate space that is her 'own', but
a Trojan horse is already within the walls, because she depends on
constant invasion to affirm her resistance. Keeping the space/time
separate becomes another manifestation of management itself. (Shortly
after this interview she had a self-confessed 'nervous breakdown'.)

Escaping Totality

The next manager we hear from is managing management, but getting
tired of it:

> I certainly take work home and I think a lot about work outside 9 to 5. And I'm
> told I think too much about it, that I'm too work-focussed. I don't mind it, but I
> notice the long-term effect that it's having. I'm actually quite exhausted at the
> minute, which is why I'm anxious to get off to Turkey and places with a
> Mediterranean feel about it [sic].

> I think it's interesting that people perceive me as working very hard. I perceive
> that I don't, and yet I know that if I stand back and look at that objectively, I do.
> Eventually you pay the price.

He does not actually *experience* management as invading. He takes work
home, thinks a lot about it outside work hours, and is not bothered by this.
But he has actually to hear from *outside* himself, from other people, that he
is being affected, that he is paying 'the price'. Then by standing back and
making an object of himself, he can see that he is overwhelmed. He now
longs for 'Turkey and places with a Mediterranean *feel*' (my emphasis),

because he is ceasing to feel himself in the space of work: he is becoming empty, disembodied, exhausted. Restoration is linked to establishing a more embodied self, in this case a feeling self. When asked whether there was a time he stopped managing he replied:

> In the kitchen or shopping. Because cooking and food is my immediate relaxation. I'm always ripping the gizzards out of a chook or stuffing it with something.

Here he comically emphasizes the aggressiveness and physicality of cooking, in contrast to the growing disembodiment of his management self. In the space of the kitchen he re-establishes a physical self through the dead body of the chicken into which, somewhat aggressively, he stuffs a new sort of life. If he can create a space and time of re-embodiment outside of management, he can go on managing. (He did, incidentally, go to Italy and Turkey, and shortly afterwards changed jobs.)

This manager's experience suggests that when management is dis-embodying, a place that is not 'managed' is necessary to restore and remember the forgotten body. But this restoration of the body is also an important factor in his being able to accurately register the effects of management itself – to actually experience his exhaustion.

The following three managers are generally satisfied with their jobs and are not feeling invaded. The first manages a health centre on the outskirts of a large city, and lives in a small town about fifty kilometres away. She affirms the value to her of a space apart from management, but expresses a stronger sense of continuity than previous managers:

> – You don't ever feel invaded by management?
> No, no. Not at all. I can switch the problems off. And I have the advantage that I live at M-, which is a forty minute drive away up the highway. No traffic. You just hop in the car and you drive home, and you work through all the bits that you haven't finished for the day. And hit the garden, and that's fine. But it's still the same person. There's a transition time. I still manage to swear at work. I swear at home, which is good.

At first she says there is an instant change. She can 'switch the problems off'. But she goes on to describe the forty minute drive to the country as 'a transition time' where unfinished management business is worked out, bringing management time to a definite end. Then she can 'hit the garden'. Note again the physical emphasis of hitting, like the ripping and stuffing of the previous manager in his kitchen. She insists, however, that the separation is not absolute: 'it's still the same person'. She gives as an example of this something she does on both sides of the transition: she swears. There is a paradox here. She is still the same person because she is not the same person. Somehow, in her case, the switching on and off maintains rather than disrupts continuity.

The next manager consciously switches off within the time of management itself. She describes this as 'time out':

– Are you always in a hurry?
  Not really. I'm very careful to use a time-out technique regularly to actually help monitor my current workload. My time out is a strategy to get through the day of doing three jobs, not just one job. Another way is . . . I have a chair position in my room. The back of it faces my desk and chair and I'll just sit down there and consciously might just breathe deeply or clench fists and then unclench fists, and it might take only two minutes, but it is a really important strategy for me if I'm feeling anxious or overwhelmed.

In line with 'sound' management practice, she is 'doing three jobs, not just one job', but the technique she describes establishes a different body within this. It is a body that faces away from the management space – the desk – and consciously ceases moving – 'I'll just sit down there'. It breathes; it tenses and relaxes its muscles. Getting re-embodied in this way re-establishes her as not 'overwhelmed'. She manages because she has an embodied experience of a reality beyond management. Like the previous manager, she can continue because she has not continued.

This manager actually refers to her practices as a 'strategy', alerting us to the possibility that the conscious use of techniques like this could be just another instance of subsuming non-management within an overall strategy of management, just like the diary technique discussed earlier. There is also that curious expression 'clench fists and then unclench fists', as though her fists were something apart from her, more like objects to be manipulated. The same could be said when she goes on to stress the importance, for her, of physical activity:

The other thing I do in relation to my workload is, I really look after myself in relation to physical activity. Unfortunately I might have days where I have a 12-hour day without a break, which is not a model to go by but if, unfortunately, that should occur, I really have to make sure to counteract that, that I do exercise.

While her 12-hour day is only half way towards Lawson's ideal, she still feels that its effects need counteracting. Once again it is the disembodying tendencies of management that require restoration of a physical sense of the self. But we must not assume that physical activity is necessarily an embodying experience. An exercise programme can end up establishing one's body as just another site to be managed. Here is a case in point from *The Cost-Conscious Manager's Toolkit*. (Auer et al., 1993: 48–9) Under Section 4.1 with its Socratic injunction 'Know Yourself', appears the following warning which by now should come as no surprise:

Initiating and managing a change process is a relentlessly lengthy, tiring and stressful business. Managers we interviewed, although showing signs of strain, demonstrated the stamina to see the process through.

Following a checklist, 'How's your physical condition?', the reader is urged to:

> Build some form of health or fitness activity into your schedule now, and give it a priority over everything else.

Why does this scheduled servicing of the body have such a different feel to that manager in his kitchen ripping the gizzards out of his chook? While the one activity restores the body to experience, the other services the machine to ensure it will last the distance. It is built in as part of a process already acknowledged as tiring and relentless. Not surprisingly, jogging or aerobics can easily become the same sort of stressful, repetitive activity as that from which they are supposed to provide relief.

With this manager however, this is probably not the case because of the way she describes the results of these techniques:

> So I found my ways of actually dealing with that situation [pressure of work] so I came to work open-faced, being able to cope with what's waiting for me whenever I step out of the lift with staff. I can't come to work thinking, I wish everyone would leave me alone so I can do my work.

She is able to be 'open-faced' when she steps out of the lift, rather than closed off and still metaphorically inside it. She can do this because she is embodied beyond the workplace even within the workplace itself. Knowing she is not totally enclosed by work means she does not have to defend herself against it. She can bring her body to work because, in some sense, it is more than at work. So her body is managing management.

Frederick Taylor was big on physical activity. His son Kempton spoke of:

> papa's oft-repeated maxim: 'Get into the game!' Whether we were of use to that football squad made little or no difference. Activity was the all-important principle, and activity was demanded as vigorous in the classroom as on the playing field. (quoted in Kakar, 1970: 167–8)

In this case activity, 'the all-important principle', reduces sport and classroom to occasions of the same.

For this manager, incessant activity marks management at its worst:

> You get bombarded with sets of issues. You're just getting order into one set and another set comes up. It's organized chaos.

These situations are manageable, however, because with practice he realizes he has access to different spaces:

> I can control when I take it [the manager's role] on much more effectively than I used to. It doesn't invade as much as it used to. That comes with practice . . . I

don't wake up at 3 o'clock in the morning and say 'I'm stopping people smiling at work'. You realize you'll find your way through those kinds of issues. You can visualize here you are in a manager's role and on the weekend you can dip down into a different kind of role, and then you come out of it. In a three weeks' holiday you can dip down much lower. You accept that it's a weekend and you can't get right down there and be really reflective. I'm happy to come up out of it.

He can visualize himself at different depths which are also marked by time. So on the *weekend* 'you can dip down into a different kind of role'. On a *three week* holiday 'you can dip down much lower'. With practice he realizes that these deeper places are always there and can be reached, although not fully on weekends. So he is 'happy to come up out of it'. That sense of other depths allows him to create a role, 'the manager's role', that is himself but is not – it can be entered and left. It is a bounded space that is not all of him; it is something that is more on the surface. So this role does not invade other spaces, like sleep at three o'clock in the morning. He realizes you can 'find your way through', rather than being over-whelmed by the bombardment of issues. Once again, as with the previous two managers, there is a sense of different times/spaces, but also a certain continuity between them, so that the effect of the other, deeper, time/space is accessible even within management. This is emphasized by the fluid metaphor, with its continuity of surface and depths.

Another interesting feature of this manager's account is that it is unclear whether those depths are in him, or he is in them. What is clear is that they are accessible as experience. Embodiment is not just being in possession of a physical body as an accompanying object. He suggests a fluidity in which an embodied sense of self crosses the boundaries between subject and object, where meaning flows from the body's immersion in what is outside it.[4] More significant than the subject/object distinction for him are distinctions between surface and depth, and between the activity of the surface and the stillness of the depths.

Excluded from Management

It would be an oversimplification to suggest that professional management is only a space of disembodiment, which must be countered by embodiment that takes place elsewhere. If management has disembodying tendencies, it can also be a space of embodiment, as some of the previous accounts show. This is often most apparent when people are excluded or locked out from management for some reason. Here is my own account of a period just before I left my last management job:

I come to work, not late but certainly not early. There are other staff there before me, as always. I feel a bit guilty about that, but not enough to change things. I make a cup of coffee and chat with L (the administrative officer) about the telly last night, and that's fine. Its part of the ritual of starting. Then I sit at my desk and look at the list I've made of things to do. There's a report to write with our six-monthly financial statement. That should be done this morning. But I don't start on that. I make a couple of phone calls, but the people aren't in. I feel discouraged by that. I look at the notes I made yesterday for the report. It would be easy to write, but I don't write it. I sit there for half an hour, doodling or thumbing through papers. I can't believe I'm so irresponsible, but there seems no more reason to write as not to write. Time seems empty – or not so much empty as numb, formless. Then L tells me we need some stock from storage. I hasten to go. It's half an hour's drive away; it's not needed immediately; a junior should go anyway, not the manager. But it's movement, and in its way at least useful. I offer to buy morning tea on the way back. I'm getting fat with morning teas, but they're filling. The day goes on like this, finding ways to fill the next expanse of time. I look forward to the end of the day, but that's not as good as it should be. It has too much to make up for.

Here it is not the demands of management that are invasive, but its emptiness. There are apparent demands – the report that has to be written – but these do not set my body moving. Neither does guilt at my inaction. Because nothing in me responds to those demands, I feel like nothing too: empty. Not only is the space of management empty, it is not there in any meaningful sense at all to me, and neither am I. I am not embodied in that space. I have to set out to make a space out of bits and pieces that refer outside of managing – coffee, chatting about the telly, food, running errands. It is a rather fragile domestic space constructed within management to fill its emptiness, but it does not really fill it. The ritual beginning to the day does not get me started. I long for the real thing, but when I get it at the end of the day, it is diminished. I am tired and there is too much demanded of it: it has to re-fashion me from nothing. It is also diminished by guilt – a sense that it is built on my role as manager, but there is no-one occupying that role. While my body comes to work, it does not work; in reality I have already left. Because I am not embodied there, I am no longer managing: no order flows from that body.

Here now is a different situation where management is prematurely terminated. In the following accounts a degree of embodiment is left behind, and the managers find themselves stranded outside it. Embodiment, once again, does not altogether coincide with physical bodies. These managers have to manage a process of recovering themselves. If this is not successful, the results can be devastating:

In a sense I've been through this before, because I was deputy at C- when the whole place was closed down. The Director then was devastated and I think it killed him. He moved to the city, but he died the next year.

In a sense the Director never recovered himself and, although he moved, he was still there in C-, in a space that was 'closed down'. This manager is now threatened with a similar situation, the closure of his own organization. I asked if he saw his previous boss's fate as a warning, and he replied:

> I suppose you could say it was. Yes, but I'm a different sort of person with more diverse interests. But I suppose it could happen to me. Time will tell.

Because this manager is embodied more diversely, he thinks he does not have so much to recover. He is, in fact, already beginning to re-identify with his original profession rather than with a career in management. He now also experiences management very differently:

> I just get a bit down; I suppose that's the best description. The past few months perhaps I've started to get a bit depressed. Less enthusiasm. I suppose a resentment about taking too much work home. Generally speaking I'm pretty committed, but I will say the gloss has gone off it. I've cut back. I used to take a lot of work home. The job is . . . when I did it anyway, a demanding job. I used to find that the only quiet time I had was at home, or at weekends. So I'd come in here roughly a day at the weekend because I felt it was the only way that I'd keep things going.

Because the job no longer keeps him 'going', he no longer feels inclined to keep it 'going'. The process of withdrawing himself from the workplace now means that work at home is experienced as invasive, whereas previously home and weekends were places where work itself could be experienced differently – a 'quiet time'. Now work is something he resists experiencing, so 'the gloss has gone off it' – it no longer shines with life. He has been excluded from its life, but he is also withdrawing the life he gave it. He has begun that work of mourning which Freud (1984) describes as a recovery of a self that was invested in another. This movement happens not only in place, where the home is being recovered for himself, but also in time. When he begins to say 'The job *is* . . .' only to shift tenses to 'when I *did* it anyway', he confirms that the 'I' that 'did it' is no longer present where the 'job is'. He no longer experiences himself fully in management, even though he is still physically there.

Our next manager describes having to recover a self that his body was locked outside of. He had moved from his previous job because it was, as he describes it, 'ticking over rather smoothly'. This almost unfelt organizational movement gave him a sense of immobility, so that, as a manager, he felt 'there wasn't a lot for me to do' – a classic problem, as we have observed, of successful management. He was looking for a position where he could 'make a difference' and 'have an effect'. When such a position came up as manager of another health centre, he describes how he 'jumped at it' – an eruption of movement that contrasted to the previous immobility. The new job promised to embody him as manager in a way the previous one had ceased to do.

Staff in the new organization, however, were not at all enthusiastic about changing, and a series of disputes escalated to a point where a Health Department representative was brought in to investigate:

I think the worst time was when 'The Inquisitor' came. That was the worst time because every day there were these meetings behind closed doors about me. It was very Star Chamber stuff. Like I was being judged, my fate was being decided, and I was excluded from the process. The irony was, there I was, the manager, but I was the person with the least power. And I found it really upsetting at the time.

While this is the place where he is embodied as manager, he cannot enter it: the 'doors' are 'closed'. In a very real sense he is being shut out from himself. Not surprisingly, this affects how he experiences himself:

I was getting physical symptoms, and getting really upset. I held together at work OK. And I fell apart for the next six months or so. And I had times when I just sort of crumbled. When I bottled it up and it was all too much. There were various times when I felt immensely depressed and teary. Yes and my soul would turn to jelly.

As management has formed his embodied experience of himself, his inability to have access to it leaves him formless. This is registered physically in his body – 'getting physical symptoms' – and in his experience of embodiment. Graphically and movingly he expresses that relationship between the order of the far-away and the order of the body. His holding himself together, bottling himself up, keeping a sense of shape, fails; tears overflow the boundaries; he falls apart, crumbles, turns to jelly. A failed order becomes a disordered, formless body.

In order to continue, he has to recover something of that self he has been excluded from – to somehow reconnect the role that gave him form with the formless emotion in which he now tends to dissolve. He does this through the help of a counsellor who is, significantly, also a management consultant who has been through a similar experience. The counsellor himself was the re-embodiment of both halves of the division:

It was a combination of wanting some technical advice and also some emotional support. Someone I could be quite open about not having to discriminate between – this is technical stuff, this is what I feel. Just someone I could say – here it all is.

To recreate a meaningful sense of self he has to bring all the pieces, without a notion of how they will fit together. But the relief in being able to present them all is also the hope that they might be made into something again, albeit differently. He has already begun the process of re-embodying himself, although he is not sure what that self might be.

Bringing Back the Body

What do these managers tell us about managing management? Management is often experienced as potentially or actually invasive. Escaping all boundary, it fills available space/time. It threatens any place where management is not, be it family, holidays, weekends or kitchen. This filling of space/time is also experienced as emptying, exhausting, disembodying. It is as though the body has no place there. Hence the maintenance of boundaries around management, of protected spaces where management is not, is important to restoring a sense of body. These spaces establish life as more than just management and, in the process, managing as more than just management. This paradoxical sense of managing goes beyond the development of countervailing activities; it actually operates within that body through which we manage success-fully. In other words, it operates within management itself. The manager is embodied within management. Let us explore further the nature of this embodiment.

To return to Lefebvre's (1991) proposition: if space is an order that comes from the body, the body and space are always in relation, even if that relation is denied. If the space of management is experienced simultaneously as full and empty, the manager is embodied as both overwhelmed and vacant. So it is strictly inaccurate to say that such a manager is disembodied. But his/her embodiment is ironically experi-enced as disembodiment. Even disembodiment has to be embodied in some way in order to be experienced at all. Successful managers, however, are embodied in a way that allows movement beyond management, even within it. The body they are in is not singular, so the space it is in does not feel singular, allowing of no other possibility but itself. It is a space that is both itself and not itself. How might we imagine such a space? Certainly differently to that abstract, singular and bounded vacancy that we know as space from geometry.[5] Georg Simmel (1994: 7), a sociologist with a remarkable capacity to discover the fundamentals of human life in quite ordinary things, offers the following account of a door:

> The human being who first erected a hut . . . revealed the specifically human capacity over against nature, insofar as he or she cut a portion out of the continuity and infinity of space and arranged this into a particular unity in accordance with a *single* meaning. A piece of space was thereby brought together and separated from the whole remaining world. By virtue of the fact that the door forms, as it were a linkage between the space of human beings and everything that remains outside it, it transcends the separation between inner and outer.

People, Simmel is saying, manage the infinitude of space by creating a space which is securely theirs, in which they can become themselves. But they are also part of that from which they are separated, and the separation only remains meaningful if there is still a connection. Hence 'the door becomes the image of the boundary point at which human beings actually always stand or can stand' (ibid.: 7). Does this not recall our earlier manager's description of herself stepping through the lift doors 'open-faced', ready to deal with the chaotic demands of the work-place because she has created herself as organized and coherent?

That earlier example also demonstrates that manageable spaces (as opposed to spaces of management) need not even be literally separate, as the image of the door might lead us to believe. The 'time out' exercises she undertook in her office happened in the same physical space as management. Imaginatively, however, they happened somewhere else: the same physical space was experienced differently. Her differently placed chair became her 'door' to a different space and a different embodiment. Equally, of course, going through a literal door may not give meaningful access to a different space, as in my own case. Even when I entered my office, it still evaded me. I was still embodied elsewhere.

The same example should also remind us, in case we have been misled by Simmel's image of hut-building, that management space is not just to be counterposed by domestic space. The issue is not where these spaces are, but how they work in relation to each other. A space can create a sense of freedom and possibility that revitalizes the order and enclosure of the hut, or it can create a sense of order and security that allows us to meet the chaos and infinity of the outside 'open-faced'. Without the connection of 'the door', either space can be experienced as a prison, or as formless and uncontrollable disorder, or, indeed, both at the same time. Without the possibility of movement, the claims of infinite demand and the enclosure of the prison actually feel the same. (Cf. Bachelard, 1969: 215) A singular space – one not articulated by a door – is not for long a space of living.

Simmel's image and the experiences of our managers open up a way beyond the mind/body, inside/outside impasse of scientific management and its modern derivatives. Simmel's door suggests that managing effectively is not a project of control, of cutting an ordered space out of the infinitude of nature, and gradually extending that order to incorporate all of nature. We saw in Taylor's case that the effect of such a project is to shut off the self that was part of the infinity of nature outside his own order. That order, then, came to feel empty and disembodied, haunted by the self that was shut out from it, while the activity of creating order remained an exhausting and undiminished struggle. However large we make the hut, there is still an infinity outside it.

The door tells us what our managers are also telling us: managing is not control of the chaos of nature from a disembodied position outside it. Rather it is an articulation of infinity and singularity, of possibility and closure, of order and disorder, of inside and outside. Our body is the locus of experience of that articulation. It is through the body that we can stand in the doorway 'open-faced', relating our order to whatever may be there outside. Through embodiment 'the human being is', in Simmel's (1994:10) words, 'the bordering creature who has no border'. If the space we create does not allow that sort of embodiment, it will not be experienced as manageable, even if we go there to manage.

While Simmel's door offers a radically different metaphor for managing than the bodiless toolkit of Chapter 1, it is also significant because it has, itself, the structure of metaphor. Metaphor, as we shall see, is a linguistic

door that articulates a connection between a singular meaning and the
infinite possibility of its connections. Managing also seems to involve an
articulation of order and possibility, suggesting a homology between
metaphor and managing. But how can a figure of speech, a trope, a
linguistic phenomenon, illuminate the sort of relationship between
embodiment and the order that flows from the body, that we have been
discussing in this chapter? If the suggested homology between metaphor
and managing is more than just fanciful it is necessary to show how a
purely linguistic phenomenon is itself embodied, and how it relates to our
capacity to order and organize.

Notes

1 One strategy that is frequently offered for managing mangement is to put it at
the service of explicit values. Management is then not just an end in itself, but is
simply a technique at the service of those values. Thus for the authors of *The Cost-
Conscious Manager's Toolkit*, their management is "values-driven" – the principal
concern being the achievement of social goals' (Auer, Repin and Roe, 1993: 9). It
should be remembered, however, that Frederick Taylor was also 'values-driven' –
both words are important here – consumed as he was with a desire for maximum
efficiency in all acts, an efficiency that he believed in turn would lead to pros-
perity, harmony, and brotherly love. Taylor was not by all accounts a religious
man, but Copley (1969: I, 72) quotes the following anecdote:

> Towards the close of his life, Mr Clark (a friend) argued to him that Scientific
> Management was the continuation and extension of the old religious truths of
> love and service. And we are informed that he nodded his head.

What distinguishes Taylor and contemporary management approaches like the
Toolkit is not a commitment to values per se, merely different values, and not even
all that different as it happens. What unites them is a belief in management as a
technology (hence the tool imagery) for achieving certain ends (social justice,
brotherly love) through the most efficient means (hence the 'cost-conscious'), a
technology which is as disembodying for values as for anything else. Unless
values can be experienced and lived rather differently, they will become part of
the problem of management, not part of the solution.

2 Time and space are related in experience (and in physics too), even though we
usually separate them conceptually. Bergson's views on this will be discussed in
Chapter 5 (see also Game, 1991, especially chapter 5).

3 This experience of something remaining at the end of the day is an affirming
experience of order, a theme that will be developed in Chapter 6.

4 Cf. Game (1991: x). 'I have found the experience of being in the sea – the
fluidity and movement in the relation between the body and the sea – very
suggestive for ways of thinking about meaning processes, and the connections
between meaning and the senses.'

5 Bachelard (1969: 47) nicely distinguishes the space of experience from the
space of geometry when he says: 'A house that has been experienced is not an inert
box. Inhabited space transcends geometrical space.'

4

MANAGING AND POETRY

Until the 1980s, coupling professional management and metaphor would seem to risk drawing Dr Johnson's indictment of metaphysical poetry as 'the most heterogeneous ideas . . . yoked by violence together'. But an interest in metaphor has become evident in management and organization theory, if not amongst managers themselves. Of particular importance has been the work of Gareth Morgan (1980, 1983, 1986), culminating in *Images of Organization*. While he has been criticized for a blindness to relations of domination in the workplace – threatening, according to one reviewer, to turn organization theory into a 'supermarket of metaphors' (Reed, 1990) – Morgan not only opened up a different way of looking at organization, but also drew attention to the ever-present working of metaphor in our thinking. His work makes it clear that being alert to metaphors not only allows us to see essential features of existing organizations, but also to explore different possibilities. Thus Kenneth Gergen (1992: 207) can ask:

> Why do we find it so congenial to speak of organizations as structures but not as clouds, systems but not songs, weak or strong but not tender or passionate?

And Tom Peters (1992: 15), less fettered by academic constraint, can state bluntly that 'today's organizational images stink'. He condemns management's obsession with Euclidean, structural metaphors because 'they miss the core of tomorrow's surviving corporation: dynamism'. 'The effective firm', he claims, 'is much more like a carnival in Rio than a pyramid along the Nile.' These writers are proposing that metaphor not only shapes our thinking, but also the ways in which we go about organizing the world. That metaphor is of relevance to management and organizational analysis is no longer controversial; the issue is: how?

Implicit in the very notion that we can pick and choose metaphors (as in a supermarket, for example) in order to get a different view of organizations is a belief in a position outside metaphor from which we can make that choice – a position of non-metaphoric or 'proper' meaning from which the usefulness of various metaphors can be compared. Metaphors are 'tools' – to use a favourite management metaphor – with which a manager/investigator can construct or discover an outside organizational reality. The issue is: which tool to choose? Reed's critique of Morgan also turns on an appeal to a reality beyond metaphor – a reality of power relations that shape the choice of metaphors that we can use or discover. Our ability to choose is ultimately limited, not by metaphor, but by a prior and more potent order of existence.

However, even as metaphor seemed to be finding its way into the organizational toolkit, postmodernity was throwing into question the whole status of that outside reality upon which the viability of, amongst other things, the toolkit metaphor itself depends. 'There is nothing out-side the text', stated Derrida (1976: 158) with an uncharacteristic and un-postmodern directness. Of all writers Derrida has been the most uncompromising in his application of the notion of textuality, claiming that all experience is textual in character. There is no point at which text can be anchored in an authentically real beyond itself, be that reality God, power relations, structure, matter or whatever. Moreover this uncompromising textuality is, in essence, metaphoric. There is no primal non-metaphoric moment when our concepts refer directly to a pre-existing reality. What we take to be a concept, Derrida argues, is a metaphor whose metaphoricity we have conveniently forgotten (1982: 251).

In the rest of this Chapter, I shall be exploring what this radical assertion of textuality and its metaphoric basis means for managing. What it does not mean is the conclusion frequently asserted by its critics: that it seeks to turn everything into undecidable language games that may be entertaining for their academic players, but are basically trivial and/or misleading for understanding, yet alone managing organization in the real world. Thus Parker (1993: 207) states that:

> it seems necessary to briefly assess the claim that nothing but language, metaphor and discourse shapes the organizational world – a central element in postmodern epistemologies. Unlike post-modernists I believe there *are* limits to human action – just because someone claims the moon is made of green cheese does not mean that, to all intents and purposes, it is.

The objective truth of the world Parker asserts, as a statement, ironically, of subjective belief, is ultimately independent of metaphor, and of language and discourse more generally. If there are no limits to textuality, he claims, then anything can become anything else, and assertion is equivalent to action.

I want to argue, however, that there is no need to posit an extra-textual 'real' to defend the relevance of the formal study of management and organization. On the contrary, a thoroughgoing understanding of the textuality and the metaphoricity of experience (and we shall shortly see how these two terms are closely related) has considerable practical bear-ing on how organization happens and how we manage our everyday and professional experience. But because there is a lot of misunderstanding about metaphor, I want to spend some time looking at how it actually works before turning to its role in managing.

Metaphor Rules

The desire to cling to a grounding reality for our experience is evident in a long tradition of thinking about metaphor, a tradition that takes as central a distinction between a proper, or literal, and a figurative meaning (Ricoeur, 1977). Literal discourse, this tradition argues, refers us to the world ruled by the law of identity: a world where X (whatever it is) is X. Metaphor on the other hand, in its assertion that something is actually something else, that X is not-X, unsettles that guarantee of identity – the guarantee that X *really* is X and not otherwise. Metaphor, in its deliberate merging of identities, would seem to undermine the very basis of truth.

Paul Ricoeur, in his stringent and meticulous study, *The Rule of Metaphor* (1977: 13), takes Aristotle's definition in the *Poetics* as a classic statement of this literal/figurative distinction:

> Metaphor consists in giving the thing a name that belongs to something else.

This definition firstly separates language from an outside world, – 'names' versus 'things' – and then places metaphor at a further remove: it is not the 'name' that properly belongs to the 'thing'. For Ricoeur there are two implications here. First, metaphor is merely a substitution of one name for another and, secondly, its effect happens at the level of the name (noun). As regards the first implication, if metaphor were merely a substitution – a name for a name – then no new information would be conveyed by it; it would just be decoration at best, and misleading at worst. Hence we have a long philosophical tradition of suspicion of metaphor, and a desire to put it in its place, subordinate to a language of reality (Le Doeuff, 1989). This suspicion is still apparent in debate around postmodernity and organization.

Ricoeur claims, on the contrary, that far from being *outside* knowledge, metaphor is the *basis* on which new knowledge is created. It is 'a talent of thinking':

> If to 'metaphorize well' is to possess mastery of resemblances, then without this power we would be unable to grasp any hitherto unknown relations between things. Therefore, far from being a divergence from the ordinary operation of language, it is the omnipresent principle of all its free action. (ibid.: 80)

What Ricoeur is suggesting is that we do not know things in themselves, but only in relation to other things, in the similarities and differences that new things have from what we already know. 'To metaphorize' is the ability to make these new relations. Without this ability, language would always be bounded by what we already know. It would have no 'free action'.

How, then, does metaphor work? This brings Ricoeur to the second implication in Aristotle's definition: that metaphor acts at the level of naming. He finds, however, the essence of metaphor not so much in the noun as in the verb – that is, in the movement between things rather than in things in themselves. A metaphor disturbs accepted meaning by setting up a tension between a literal 'is not' and a metaphorical 'is', transforming assertions of fixity and singularity into processes of becoming and possibility (Game and Metcalfe 1996: 50).

Let us look at this operation in a brief but nevertheless profoundly philosophical poem by the fifteenth century Japanese poet Ikkyu (in the translation by Stryk and Ikemoto, 1981: 72). The poem is remarkable not only because it works metaphorically, but because it is itself an account of metaphor and an account of the metaphoricity of being:

VOID IN FORM

When, just as they are,
White dewdrops gather
On scarlet maple leaves,
Regard the scarlet beads!

Ikkyu's poem asserts that the 'white dewdrops' and 'scarlet maple leaves' are 'just as they are', that X is X, an assertion of identity. But at that very moment, and in the same space, they are also something else – 'scarlet beads'. X is also not-X. The metaphor not only enables us to grasp a new relation between things, but also makes us wonder at how something can be and not be at the same time, a wonder that is generalized in the poem's title, 'VOID IN FORM'. For something to be something else at the same time, it must both have its own form and yet be void – have no form at all so it can receive another. In giving the poem this title, Ikkyu shows how metaphor confronts us with the idea that there is something essentially contradictory in form itself. In Ricoeur's (1977: 255) formulation:

there is no other way to do justice to the notion of metaphorical truth than to include the critical incision of the literal 'is not' within the ontological vehemence of the [metaphorical] 'is'.

But this is all very well for poetry, it may be argued, a realm where the moon is green cheese. Such flights of fancy are alien to the down-to-earth (or moon) world of management – or are they? Consider this manager's response to the question, 'Do you have an image of the organization'?

Well, yes. I sort of believe it is a bit like a round orange with cinnamon sticks on one side, which are a nice group of people – people prepared to work collaboratively, respect each other, work together. I sort of get a dark picture coming on the other side. You could sort of start to scrape and peel some of the orange peel off. And that's the other half of the organization – all organizations have them, but there's that small group of people, difficult, who don't want to work with organizations.

This manager locates her sense of being in her organization through her experience of food. A feeling of wholeness and totality is evoked by an orange, whose roundness she specifies. The people she likes, who will work well together, evoke the pervasive fragrance of her favourite spice. The visibility of the orange conversely evokes a dark side which is not visible, and where lurk 'that small group of people' who nevertheless loom in her mind as the other half of the orange, one she would like 'to scrape and peel'.

This manager's response evokes a lively sense of how she experiences her organization. In describing it in this way, she is living it, and allowing us, through our own experience of oranges and cinnamon sticks, scraping and peeling, to live her satisfactions and frustrations. But the process by which she does this is strange to say the least. Here is a world where everything is something else: a workplace is an orange; people are cinnamon sticks; disciplining and sacking are peeling and scraping. Here is metaphor at work, the very essence of poetry.

'A Buzzing World'

Metaphor asserts that an entity itself both is and is not. This is to claim much more than a trick or ornament of language. Ricoeur goes so far as to speak of 'metaphorical truth'. But can a metaphor be true? If truth is defined as establishing identity – that X *is* really X – then metaphor cannot be true by definition. But Ikkyu and Ricoeur are challenging that notion of truth. We can only know X, they are suggesting, by experiencing its relation with not-X. For Ricoeur (1977: 254) a successful metaphor is:

> an experience in which the creative dimension of language is consistent with the creative aspects of reality itself. Can one create metaphors without believing them and without believing that, in a certain way, 'that is'?

Whitehead (1978: 50) attempted to express this reality, which implies the interdependence of all identities, in his principle of universal relativity:

> according to this principle an actual entity is present in other actual entities. In fact if we allow for degrees of relevance, and for negligible relevance, we must say that every actual entity is present in every other actual entity.

What we normally think of as objects, according to Whitehead, are abstracted simplifications of actual entities:

objectification relegates into irrelevance, or into a subordinate relevance, the full constitution of the objectified entity. Some real component of the objectified entity assumes the role of being how that particular entity is a datum in the experience of the subject. (ibid.: 62)

The constitution of an objective world to a subject, a world in which everything has its proper meaning, where X is X and not-X is not-X, is something of an illusion, an illusion that:

> does violence to that immediate experience which we express in our actions, our hopes, our sympathies, our purposes, and which we enjoy in spite of our lack of phrases for its verbal analysis. We find ourselves in a buzzing world, amid a democracy of fellow creatures; whereas under some disguise or other, orthodox philosophy can only introduce us to solitary substances, each enjoying an illusory experience. (ibid.: 49–50)

It is to this 'buzzing world' – 'buzzing' suggesting both aliveness and movement – that metaphor restores us, and metaphor is able to do so, not through some trick of language, but because it is, in Ricoeur's (1977: 254) words, 'consistent with the creative aspects of reality itself'.[1]

Metaphor works because, quite simply, that is how the world comes. Language is not, in this account, a mysterious activity outside of reality yet referring to it. Textuality and the world are not separate things. But this does not mean that all metaphor works, and Whitehead's concept of degrees of relevance allows us to address Parker's objection about the moon and green cheese. If any 'is' is implicated in the whole of 'is-not'[2], then we are obliged to admit that the moon and green cheese are implicated in one another in some way. But from our current situation, preoccupations and experience, these implications do not do much to enrich our sense of 'moon'. This does not mean that 'moon' is a self-identity whose boundaries are fixed and can never include those implications in a more meaningful way. But currently we can acknowledge Parker's example as a metaphor of trivial interest to our experience. All metaphor generates knowledge, but not all metaphor generates relevant knowledge.

Metaphor as Embodied Experience

That last assertion suggests a question: relevant to whom? Answering this question introduces another aspect of metaphor whose absence from discussion has tended to limit debates around metaphor and organization. Alvesson (1993: 116), for example, states that a 'metaphor allows an object to be perceived and understood from the viewpoint of another object'. In its account of metaphor as a relation between two different terms this follows Richards, 1936 ('tenor' and 'vehicle'), Black, 1962 ('focus' and 'frame'), Lakoff and Johnson, 1980 ('source' and 'target'), and, indeed, our argument so far has also, through Ricoeur, followed this structure ('X' and 'not-X'). But, returning for the moment to the question of whether or not metaphor is true, the poet Wordsworth (1800: 16) offers an answer that alerts us to a third 'term'. Writing at the beginning of the nineteenth century when poetry was less socially marginal than it is now, he has no qualms in declaring that the object of poetry is indeed truth; but that the truth of poetry is:

> not individual and local, but general and operative; not standing upon external testimony, but carried alive into the heart by passion.

This declaration of Wordsworth's raises an aspect of metaphor that has also been noted by Ricoeur. Metaphor is an *experience*. It is 'carried alive into the heart by passion'. In Ikkyu's poem, it is not a logical proposition that he is presenting to us, it is an invitation to share in a moment of discovery:

> *Regard the scarlet beads!*

The poem convinces only if we acknowledge the experience. Otherwise it is so many words. No new knowledge is produced.

If metaphoric experience produces knowledge, it does not do so by placing a disembodied observer in front of an external object. We as experiencing subjects are situated in, and implicated in, the knowledge that is produced. Metaphor, then, involves three 'terms'; or, perhaps more accurately, that third 'term', our experience, is the realization of the connection implicit in the other two.[3] Merleau-Ponty (1974: 106) has characterized this knowledge as 'truth in the situation':

> As long as I cling to the ideal of an absolute spectator, of knowledge with no point of view, I can see my situation as nothing but a source of error. But if I have once recognized that through it I am grafted on to every action and all knowledge which can have a meaning for me, and that step by step it contains everything that can exist for me, then my contact with the social in the finitude of my situation is revealed to me as the point of origin of all truth, including scientific truth. And since we have an idea of truth, since we are in truth and cannot escape it, the only thing left for me to do is to define a truth in the situation.

If, in Whitehead's terms, every entity is implicated in every other, then we cannot escape that web of implication either. We only know from within our experience. And that experience implies embodiment. I am there, not just 'mentally', but in my whole body, as T.S. Eliot (1963: 290) observes when discussing the sort of poetry he likes:

> Those who object to the 'artificiality' of Milton or Dryden, sometimes tell us to 'look into our hearts and write'. But that is not looking deep enough; Racine or

Donne looked into a good deal more than the heart. One must look into the cerebral cortex, the nervous system, and the digestive tract.

It is not from the point of a mind contained within a body, but through our body that we not only feel, but also think: we *experience*. Hence, for Donne, in Eliot's account, 'a thought . . . was an experience'. It was as immediate 'as the odour of a rose' (ibid.: 287). Or, as Merleau-Ponty (1964: 162) puts it when speaking of a different art:

> The painter 'takes his body with him', says Valéry. Indeed we cannot imagine how a mind could paint. It is by lending his body to the world that the artist changes the world into paintings. To understand these transubstantiations we must go back to the working, actual body – not the body as a chunk of space or a bundle of functions but that body that is an intertwining of vision and movement.

To paint, to write poetry, and, I shall argue, to manage well, requires us to think metaphorically. Metaphoric thinking implies embodiment because embodiment is how we are implicated in the multifarious possibilities of connection that take us beyond what we already know. But to be embodied in a situation is also to take part in the metaphoricity of all the entities within it, to be part of that 'democracy of fellow creatures' that, in Whitehead's very radical account, extends far beyond political or workplace democracy. To be constituted metaphorically is to have one's identity open to implication in everything beyond it; it is, in answer to Hamlet's question, to be *and* not to be.

Metaphor and Organization

But how does being metaphorically embodied in a situation relate to its management? In the same essay already referred to, T.S. Eliot (1963: 287) contrasts ordinary and poetic experience:

> the ordinary man's experience is chaotic, irregular, fragmentary. The latter falls in love, or reads Spinoza, and these two experiences have nothing to do with each other, or with the noise of the typewriter or the smell of cooking; in the mind of the poet these experiences are always forming new wholes.

Ordinary experience tends to be chaotic and fragmentary, but poetic experience is organized and connected because it is alert to the implication of things in each other. Metaphor forms chaotic and disconnected experiences into new wholes. A metaphoric talent is also, then, a talent for *organization*. Poets have a highly developed capacity for creating organization in experience, but here Eliot's formulation is very suggestive: in the mind of the poet 'these experiences are always forming new wholes'. It is the experiences that organize, not the poet who organizes from somewhere outside experience.

Ordinary experience tends to be chaotic and fragmented, but poetic experience organizes and connects. It allows us to form 'new wholes'. Eliot speaks of the 'mind' of the poet, but he makes it clear that this is an embodied mind. Thought for a poet, Eliot contends, is 'an experience'. It is as immediate 'as the odour of a rose' (Eliot 1961: 278). The poet's 'mind' can organize in this way only because all the senses are involved in thought. Embodiment is the way we are implicated in the multifarious possibilities of connection that take us beyond what we already know. Embodiment 'lends' our body to the world by allowing the world to enter into our experience.

To enable disconnected experiences to form 'new wholes' requires that the poet be within those experiences, exhibiting a certain openness of body to let them develop through him/her, because it is the experiences that organize, not the poet who organizes from somewhere outside experience. The critic F.R. Leavis (1963) describes this openness of body when distinguishing the different readings demanded by literary and philosophic texts. Literary texts, Leavis (1963: 213) argues, differ from philosophy in demanding 'a fuller-bodied response', an opening of one-self to all the possibilities of the text. Leavis elaborates this as a different relationship to the 'object' under consideration:

> Philosophy, we say, is 'abstract' . . . and poetry 'concrete'. Words in poetry invite us, not to 'think about and judge' but to 'feel into' or 'become' – to realize a complex experience that is given in the words. They demand, not merely a fuller-bodied response, but a completer responsiveness – a kind of responsiveness that is incompatible with the judicial, one-eye-on-the-standard approach suggested by Dr Wellek's phrase: 'your norm with which you measure every poet'. (ibid.: 212–13)

To 'realize' the text, 'a complex experience that is given in words', is not a matter of measuring or judging it from outside that experience, but experiencing what is there, entering it and letting it enter one's body. Such a process of experiencing is not just a passive absorption into the situation, but also a participation in a process of organization. Realizing the experience, embodying it, claims Leavis, relates it to other experiences that are also embodied, so that 'a certain value is implicit in the realizing' (ibid.: 213). This sense of relative valuation is an ordering of experience. By comparison, Leavis finds that attempting to summarize his method as a system of rules is, in fact, disorganizing:

> I feel that by my own methods I have attained a relative precision that makes this summarizing seem intolerably clumsy and inadequate. (ibid.: 215)

Leavis is here talking about literary texts, Eliot about poetry and Merleau-Ponty about painting. But the postmodern extension of the notion of textuality to experience in general invites the transfer of these insights beyond the formally containing barriers of the arts. Reading for

Barthes (1986: 13), as for Leavis, means being open to a text in a way that lets its organization work in our body: 'to read is to make our body work . . . at the invitation of the text's signs', but that 'text' can be a photograph, a building or a landscape. The issue is a relation between the body and that which is beyond it. Barthes characterizes this embodied reading, like Leavis, as a response to an invitation. Such a response, with its implications of graciousness, courtesy, respect, openness and, perhaps, a certain tentativeness, is a far remove from the dominating self-assurance and detached calculation of the heroes of much management literature.

Reading from the Body

But how might a manager engage in an embodied reading? Two contrasting accounts follow from managers of community health services in the Australian State of Queensland. Each manager had begun her current job after moving from another State, so that both had to deal with a new environment. Here is the first:

> – Do you spend a lot of time in the office?
> I like to get around. And then to have a total day in the office. I make a point of whichever areas I'm involved in at least going to a staff meeting at least once a month. If there's something going on, I'll go much more regularly. Sometimes I'll just wander in. They're very welcoming at R-; sometimes I'll just wander in there. People know that I'm available. People are often phoning, calling in. So I have a sense of being very close, and they tell me that I am, that I'm accessible. And that's part of the job.

Some of this manager's activity could be seen as purely instrumental: gathering information, going to staff meetings where 'there's something going on'. But some of the movement comes across as less directed: 'sometimes I'll just wander in'; 'I like to get around'. Nor can this be put down to random surveillance, keeping people on their toes through its unpredictability. There is a sense of pleasure in moving within the organization: 'They're very welcoming at R-; sometimes I'll just wander in there.' This sense of being close to, and accessible by, the organization is not just arbitrary either. She is convinced that 'that's part of the job'.

While her job is geographically dispersed, she exhibits the same involvement during 'a total day in the office':

> I've got a wheel on the door that says whether I'm available or do not disturb or out. If somebody wants to make an appointment they would do it with J [her secretary]. They don't have to do that. They can wait in the corridor and I'll see them, or just come and bang on the door. I walk around the place a lot. The admin area's a good place because that's a continual crossing over space. I like to get caught up in conversations and stuff. The tea room's another good place.

The wheel on the door indicates degrees of openness. But staff are not just engaged by the manager in her own space and in her own way: there are a range of opportunities for contact, particularly in neutral 'crossing over space'. Again there is a sense of pleasure in engagement that is not just active and controlling. She allows the environment to work on her: 'I like to get *caught up* in conversations and stuff.' She lends her body to the new situation, and it lends itself to her. She is open to its invitation, and so, while admitting to still finding Queensland 'something of a culture shock', she seems to have made a successful transition between the old and the new situations, to the extent of feeling comfortable and even enjoying her present position.

Now consider the case of a second manager who also came to Queensland from a southern state, bringing with her what she thought were 'reasonably modern management practices'. It took, she said, 'a fairly contentious eighteen months' to realize that 'something was going wrong':

> It was about coming to Queensland; it's like being in another world, only it didn't really hit me at first. I'd just keep running into brick walls and I didn't know why. Things are very laid back here. You come to work and go into the staff room and start talking about some problem at work and people just look at you. They're talking about what's on TV last night or something. They just won't talk about work things straight away, and if you do you're made to feel that's wrong. I don't watch those shows and I'm not interested in talking about them. But you've got to, to some extent. Pretend you're not interested in the job.
> – Anything else?
> Well . . . it's not just staff. Like it doesn't seem to matter if someone can do the job or not. They just tell you, 'So-and-so's a good bloke.' If he's a 'good bloke,' that's what matters most. But I like to see the job done. That's why I'm there. So until I worked it out it seemed like everyone was conspiring against me. It's still hard. I don't like putting on an act.

This manager never left her southern identity with its 'reasonably modern management practices' so that, while coming to Queensland, she was still embodied 'outside' it, to the extent that it felt like 'running into brick walls'. Even when she eventually worked out that the organization was not what she thought it was, she felt she could only bridge the gap in a manipulative way – 'putting on an act' – which did not make her feel comfortable. She wanted to be in control, and yet separate – thinking about and judging, in Leavis' terminology, rather than feeling into and becoming. Her body was not open to the invitation of her new situation, so only misunderstanding and disruption resulted. She shortly afterwards resigned from that job.

'A Growing Stability of Organization'

How does making one's body work within the textuality of the workplace lead, in Leavis' phrase, to 'a growing stability of organization'? How does it allow one to manage? Here is one manager's account of what is generally a difficult and much avoided process for managers, dismissing a member of staff. This is a remarkable interview. Usually when you ask managers why they had to dismiss someone, they give organizational reasons like 'refused reasonable requests', 'stole money', 'forged time-sheets', and the like, measuring errant behaviour against an outside standard. What they rarely give is an account of how this behaviour comes to be experienced as disruptive. The experience usually vanishes in rationalized and disembodied accounts of the incident.[4] This manager is very unusual in being able to take her *experience* of this incident seriously. This enables her to give an embodied account of it – a non-rationalized memory – however strange it might sound to the rational mind.

Her first sense of a problem with this particular staff member was something of a cliche of embodiment:

> – How did you first notice something was wrong?
>   There's a gut reaction first off.

A problem is registered in her 'gut'. But the phrase 'gut reaction' is such a cliche that the actual experience of it is usually left unexamined. When I asked her to elaborate, however, her 'gut reaction' proliferated metaphorically in quite a complex manner:

> It's almost a visual concept. This is going to sound quite crazy. It's almost a visual concept of an environment, and you're starting to realize part of the environment is beginning to react negatively to the other parts of the environment. It's that there's an onflowing . . . almost going in a wave-like motion. It's like my budget concept. It's not there in dollars and cents but there almost like a bar diagram gone wrong. I know how every programme should be relevant to where the actual budget is. I don't know the breakdown to the last cent. I guess in the people management it's similar. You've sort of got a picture all the time in your head and you become aware of tension going to build because of that.

The internal, 'gut' reaction becomes visual and extends out to the environment – 'It's almost a visual concept of an environment.' The disturbed environment becomes a movement in which she participates – 'It's that there's an onflowing . . . almost going into a wave-like motion.' Because the environmental picture is still 'in [her] head' it allows her to experience 'where the tension is going to build'. An environmental disturbance re-organizes her body in an uncomfortable way. She relates this discomfort to a disturbance in her budget, something she also registers as an embodied experience. The 'bar diagram' is not a piece of paper for her, but a part of herself that lets her experience the relation between different programmes.

If this sounds muddled, it is because this manager is trying to articulate something that our usual geometry of the body and space doesn't allow

– how inside and outside are permeable, flow together, and sometimes change places. There is movement between them that allows change in the outside to be also a bodily experience, not just a conclusion deduced from evidence. Not only inside and outside, but the senses that we separate in thought – vision, feeling – in experience flow into and substitute for one another.[5] A gut feeling is a picture, is a movement, is a tension. Because this manager is metaphorically identified in the situation, she can develop, in Leavis' words, 'a fuller-bodied response' that will let her 'realize as sensitively and completely as possible this or that which claims [her] attention'.

But as yet no particular meaning has emerged beyond a sense of unease, an anticipation of possible future disorder whose traces are present in the world around her. When I ask her to go on, she begins to locate an 'external' problem that correlates to the more 'internal' one as she speaks about moving into the corridor. This corridor is a space that belongs to no-one, but where people overlap in a less structured way:

> Well, just walking down the corridor at work you become aware that there's tension in the air, or that things are getting sharper. . . . Some part of the mental picture's beginning to malfunction, like a red light going on on the electrical board or something.

Here she experiences 'tension in the air' – outside – that corresponds to 'a red light going on' in a mental picture – inside. An inside and an outside are starting to more clearly define themselves.

At this point, for the first time, another staff member materializes in the account, but note how his presence is registered by her body: it is a touch that is distinctly uncomfortable:

> With him I started to realize it was certainly starting to rub. Some people might come in for a day and be more withdrawn or abrasive to somebody, and that's O.K. for a day. When it's been a week you ferret around a little and find out why.

The continued abrasion prompts her to explore the outside more actively, 'to ferret around a little'. She starts speculating on a reason for the problem:

> It may be something's happened in their house, their relationship's going to break down

Why does she look first for this sort of reason? This relates to the way order is embodied for her, and why she experiences this staff member as disorderly. Earlier in the interview, when I had asked her where she learned about management, she replied, as women managers often do, that she had to manage her own family:

> I manage my children, if you call it that, very much the same way as I manage work in a way. Because I operate in a single parent status I feel responsible at home the same way as at work. The responsibility doesn't change wherever you go.

Having a family embodies her sense of what responsibility feels like. Her bodily sense of disturbance, her 'gut reaction', starts to emerge as a disturbance of that sense of responsibility by the offending staff member. This in turn offers a possible explanation for disturbing behaviour when she speculates that 'something's happened in their house'. But 'their house' is also the workplace where 'something's happened' and where 'a relationship's going to break down' – the relationship between her and the staff member. Once again her body relates experiences of different places in order to make sense (and I mean that in both sensual and intellectual senses) of what is going on. She is not just passively absorbing a situation, but is also bringing to it experiences of other situations. This is not happening in a deliberate or conscious way, but through the process of realizing the situation as sensitively and completely as possible. Her 'reading' of the textuality of the organization is, again following Leavis, 'a process of relating and organizing'.

It is only at this point that she starts to refer to explicit organizational problems, because they only now have meaning in the context of her sense of order. They offend her sense of responsibility. She continues:

> He was the sort of guy who needed a little more supervision than most. If he thought he could get away with something he would. He fiddled his time sheets and things like that. And that was something first brought to my attention by the administrative officer. I had a bit of a chat to him about that and it went away.

The informal 'bit of a chat' rather than a formal interview suggests an attempt to keep the problem within the family, as it were. At first this seems to work, but then he resists being re-incorporated:

> Then he seemed quite cut off, and a couple of clients requested to be transferred. So I had a bit of a chat and he didn't think I should be enquiring into his personal life, and that was fine.

The next stage, minuted interviews, begins a formal separation from the 'family'. What brings this on is an apparently trivial incident that metaphorically has considerable significance:

> He was always someone who claimed more than anyone else and that was within his right, so I didn't have a go at him about that. At that stage we had financial cuts and everyone was being a bit restrained. One of the last straws, and it seems ridiculous, but he put in a petty cash claim for his pencil leads!

She begins by saying he was 'someone that claimed more than anyone else', but adds that that was 'within his right'. Why should the petty cash claim then, apparently so trivial in itself, go beyond his right? Why was this the incident that she chose to recount as critical? I was struck by the sexual inference of the claim for pencil leads. (*The Dinkum Dictionary: A Ripper Guide to Aussie English*, p. 331 *'put lead in your pencil* [of men] increase sexual performance: e.g., This drink will put lead in your pencil!') I thought this interpretation was getting a bit wild, so I prompted her explicitly:

– Sounds very Freudian, claiming lead for his pencil.

She had no hesitation in accepting this:

It sure was!

A claim that from outside 'seems ridiculous', metaphorically condenses her growing sense of disorder. By wanting the organization to symbolically supply his manhood, he abrogates any sense of responsibility. But by wanting the family mother to put lead in his pencil, he also symbolically violates the incest taboo, thus becoming 'someone who claimed more than anyone else'. From this point he can no longer be contained within her embodied sense of order.

This manager's account, whatever else it does, reveals her participation in Whitehead's 'democracy of fellow creatures'.[6] Waves, her budget, the corridor at work, her family, red lights, electrical boards, rubbing, time sheets, the errant staff member, pencil leads, incest: all these enter into an emerging experience of disorder, and they can do so because through her body she participates in them and they in her. Through this participation she is implicated in a process of increasing organization of the work space, beginning with an internal unease and progressing to an increasing externalization of the problem to the point where it cannot be managed within that space. This externalization coincides with a sense of ultimate affront to an embodied experience of order around which her other perceptions and intuitions become organized. It is not the specific metaphors of family and incest that are of such interest here as metaphoricity itself: the embodiment of relations, that creates a dynamic sense of order and disorder and 'a growing stability of organization'. This ordering does not come about by imposing a meaning from outside the situation. Rather the 'truth in the situation', in Merleau-Ponty's phrase, emerges from being embodied within it. It is developed in and through experience.

While this account seems strange from a rationalized perspective of management, I would contend that any management action comes about through some such process as this, otherwise no action would come about at all. We stated earlier that this manager's sense of unease was a 'bodily experience, not just a conclusion deduced from evidence'. But really, a conclusion deduced from evidence only moves us if it is also a bodily experience. Similarly, breaking an organizational rule, such as fiddling a time sheet, only instigates a disciplinary procedure if it is experienced by someone as disruptive. It must offend an embodied sense of order in a way that cannot be contained. Every day in management we see some rule-breaking that is tolerated, and some that is not. The rule itself gives no account of how it is offensive for one person and less so, or not at all, for another. It is only when we experience the rule through our bodies that it can move us in one direction or another.

This manager, I contend, manages metaphorically. In doing this she does not, however, use metaphor as a management 'tool' to modify an organizational situation in a pre-conceived direction. Rather, she has an embodied openness to experience that allows organization to happen from within her situation, rather than being imposed from outside or on top of it. But abandoning an instrumental relation to a perceived outside reality does not result in a situation of undecidability where anything can be anything else. On the contrary, it creates organization and allows her to manage, because metaphor relates her, through her body, meaningfully to the world.

Notes

1 We can, in fact, turn the tables on literal and transparent language, as Game and Metcalfe (1996: 46) do with sociological texts, suggesting that the literal is itself a rhetorical manoeuvre:

> The empirical material presented in sociological texts is not a presentation of the raw world but a rhetorical manoeuvre encouraging readers to accept the text's plausibility and authenticity. It operates like period furniture in realist theatre, to reassure us rhetorically that we are facing the world directly, without the deceit of rhetoric.

Equally we can argue that down-to-earth managers, for whom facts are facts, are rhetorically convincing themselves that they alone live in the real, unmediated world. In doing this they are living in a world as abstract as that of any philosopher.

2 Cf. Whitehead (1978: 11): 'every proposition proposing a fact must, in its complete analysis, propose the general character of the universe required for that fact. There are no self-sustained facts, floating in nonentity'.

3 Bachelard (1969: 100) gives a striking and succinct formulation of the way this 'third term' undoes the object world and its representations:

> Thus values alter facts. The moment we love an image, it cannot remain the copy of a fact.

4 This post hoc rationalization of experience, of course, creates methodological problems in interviewing, because the original experience may now only be available in its rationalized form.

5 This constant fluidity of logical boundaries leads to constantly mixed metaphors. Literary strictures against mixed metaphor may well be an injunction to take metaphor seriously as thought, but they also represent rationality's last-ditch attempt to police metaphor: if it is going to be permitted, it must at least be consistent. The nature of metaphor itself, however, resists such attempts to nail it down.

6 It may be argued that the term 'democracy' should be taken here with something of a grain of salt, as the non-democratic hierarchy of the workplace privileges the manager as the defining site of organization and major determinant of the outcome. The staff member, after all, is in no position to dismiss her. Certainly the way formal organizations are set up may cut across or vitiate the sort of organizational potential we are discussing here. The issue here is that, given this staff/management relationship, how is it actually lived from the perspective of the manager?

5

MANAGING AND ORDER

In the last chapter, I examined the metaphorical character of managing. Metaphor requires an embodied openness that allows previously disparate elements to form new wholes. The manager in our last example allows her body to read the space in which she works. In fact, she reads this space as a text if we take Barthes' characterization of text as not 'a line of words, releasing a single "theological" meaning, the intention of a God-Author' (1986: 52), but:

> the simultaneous multiplicity of meanings, of points of view, of structures, a space extended outside the laws which prescribe contradiction (Text is the very postulation of such a space). (ibid.: 42)

In reading her workplace, she does not scan it to release a single meaning. She does not immediately jump to conclusions or try to resolve the ambiguity with which the space presents her. She allows meaning to develop through her involvement in this space, rather than prematurely closing it off.

Nevertheless she does eventually close things off. The process as she describes it does lead to a definite conclusion – the dismissal of the unsatisfactory staff member. Her institution of a grievance procedure, with its minuted interviews, is in fact designed to compel a single meaning and to allow an explicit decision to dismiss or not dismiss. Moreover, she states quite emphatically that she was 'very glad' when there were minuted interviews. She experienced them as liberating. Managing, it seems, involves singularity and closure as well as multiplicity and openness. But where does this leave our argument about metaphor? Is the metaphoric simply a stage in the managing process – a stage for whose completion we have to look elsewhere?

Managing Metaphor

Philosophical debates around metaphor, in fact, often take that line of argument, acknowledging metaphor's value, but only within the framework of an encompassing 'higher' order. In the last chapter we saw Ricoeur as the champion of metaphor, but that is not the whole story. While he finds metaphor to be the essence of creativity in language, he finds it problematic to locate metaphor, as Derrida (1982) for example does, as the basis of all thought. This, Ricoeur argues, is because metaphor, even while creating meaning, also disrupts it. Because X is also not-X, meaning at the metaphoric level is essentially unstable and undecidable:

> The resulting gain in meaning (of metaphorical utterance) is thus not yet a *conceptual* gain, to the extent that the semantic innovation is not separable from the switching back and forth between the two readings, from their tensions and from the kind of stereoscopic vision this dynamism produces. (ibid.: 296)

Discourse, Ricoeur admits, certainly begins in the metaphorical realm of ambiguity 'when we dismantle the reign of objects in order to let be and, to allow to be uttered, our primordial belonging to a world which we inhabit' (ibid.: 306). This is Whitehead's 'buzzing world'. However, it is only at the *conceptual* level, Ricoeur argues, that a metaphoric gain in meaning is stabilized. With the concept we move definitively beyond metaphor to enter a world of decidable meaning that makes rigorous thinking and reflection possible. This is a world where X remains X. With the emergence of the conceptual, metaphor, in a phrase that links Ricoeur's philosophical argument with the discourse on management, is no longer, 'absolutely uncontrollable'. The conceptual becomes, in effect, a management strategy for metaphor.

An analagous management strategy has been suggested by Tsoukas (1993: 342) for utilizing metaphor in the study of organizations. While acknowledging metaphor's potential in this field he laments the absence of methodology that would develop metaphors to yield firm organizational knowledge. He proposes a 'structure mapping' theory of analogy by which metaphors provide the initial insight into potentially more systematic parallels between two domains, which are then explored by a process of analogical reasoning. This process, Tsoukas claims, allows 'the progressive constitution of a more powerful explanatory language in the form of abstractions'. Metaphor is by this means harnessed to 'a creative way of generating scientific knowledge about organizational phenomena'.

Proceeding by analogy, we could acknowledge, in our staff dismissal example, the validity of that openness and immersion in a world of 'primordial belonging' that the manager exhibits as the problem begins to emerge. The moment of true management, however, occurs when an explicit procedure raises the situation out of this undecidable metaphoric soup and elicits a clear outcome.

All these strategies exhibit a decided unease about a domain where nothing is finally fixed or settled and where meaning is always multiple. They accept metaphor, but only on condition that it is contained within, or restrained by, a higher and more abstract order. This conditional acceptance of metaphor, however, threatens to return us to the world of management explored in Chapter 1. Ricoeur, revealingly, speaks of the 'distancation' of his conceptual or speculative realm as being created by a necessity that proceeds 'from the very structures of the mind' (Ricoeur, 1977: 300). The 'primordial world' of metaphoric sensuality is controlled through a process of disembodiment that reproduces the mind/body split as a split between speculative and metaphoric discourse. In the case of Tsoukas, with a more management orientation, metaphor is something to be 'harnessed' as a 'creative way for generating scientific knowledge', much as Heidegger described the Rhine being harnessed as a way of generating power. What was, like nature, disturbing and unsettling, can now be mastered and made useful by a process of increasing abstraction from the sensual.

Metaphor and Order

Can we then think of order in the context of metaphor without reverting to a process of disembodied control? Can we produce a singular, precise, bounded meaning that does not deny the fluidity, the relationality, and the multiplicity of metaphor? Some postmodern management commentators would assert the impossibility of such a project (Peters, 1992), and hence the impossibility of any order that is not a mask for control and manipulation (Burrell, 1992). But before either abandoning or succumbing to the project of management, let us attend more closely to the way our manager describes her arrival at that moment of singularity and closure, the minuted meetings that signalled entry into a formal dismissal procedure. She does not talk about it in a way that is essentially different from the rest of her account. It is something that still happens within embodied experience: she feels 'very glad'. Reaching this point both moves her, and allows her to move within the situation, while not negating her previous experience. It is continuous with it, while at the same time being discontinuous. She moves, but not into a realm that is utterly distant from whence she came. She has not, I would argue, left the realm of metaphor. Why not?

Recalling Simmel's metaphor for metaphor – the door between the multifarious possibility of outside and the secure and bounded closure of inside – the image is not one of two opposed spaces, as in multiplicity versus singularity, or metaphor versus concept. It is an image of spaces in relation: metaphor is the door. It is the articulation of the closure of the hut with the infinity beyond it, of the clarity of the concept with the dynamism of meaning that it would seek to hold and pin down, of the singularity of order with the multiplicity of possibility. Understood in this way, order, concept, singularity, when they work as experience, work within a metaphoric structure.

For our manager, entry into a formal procedure allows her to now experience herself in relation to the multiplicity of meaning in which she is initially immersed. She can then move within that multiplicity in a singular way. She becomes ordered. This order, however, must relate to multiplicity, or no movement will be possible. The two domains must be in relation to one another, each animating the other in a way that will allow action to proceed. This manager embodies singularity, but singularity within multiplicity, so she feels the arrival at minuted interviews as an organizing moment.

The Paradox of Order

I now want to explore this metaphoric working of order and singularity through a management activity that seems to epitomize the desire to evoke a singular meaning: planning. Planning evokes a surprising range of responses from managers.[1] Here, for instance, the mere mention of planning elicits vehement rejection:

> That's all shit. You spend all your energy serving the plan.

For this manager, a plan actually creates disorder: it is 'shit'. A plan draws away energy from freedom to manage as he sees fit.

Another manager finds planning essential:

> I do think you need a well documented [business plan] . . . to say this is where you're going, because it gives people direction. It stops them feeling that they've got this sort of vacant, open void.

For this manager a plan enables navigation in an otherwise formless void. In doing so it stops them feeling that they are that void. A plan, in giving direction, gives shape and substance: it is an embodying process.

A third manager is neither as dismissive as the first nor so enthusiastic as the second. She uses planning to get 'outside' the day-to-day flow of events:

> When I presented today that we achieved 70 per cent of the actual plan, that's extra activities. It's not the day-to-day stuff, but things we want to change or are reviewing or are doing differently.

Here formal planning creates 'space' for movement at the margin of a day that would otherwise seem completely filled. However, she also feels planning's potential to exclude her from a space of managing:

> I don't want to end up being a recluse in my office, being a planning or paper machine . . . You need to have things on the pulse and be with people. That's my dilemma. I don't want to give up those that I've got organized because of those structures . . .

This manager thinks of planning as being in opposition to life, – to being 'on the pulse', to being 'with people'. As she needs 'to have things on the pulse' in order to manage, planning can be disruptive, she feels, of what 'I've got *organized*'. Planning, for her, has potential to be *disorganizing* as well as organizing.

That opposition between planning and life seems reflected by managers in their own lives. Very few of the managers I interviewed, even those enthusiastic about planning, actually planned to become managers. Typical of answers to the question 'How did you get into management?' are the following:

> I tumbled into it actually.
> Er, drifted I suppose is the best description.
> I think because it's what inevitably happens in this area if you want to get promoted.
> Probably by default.
> I think I just evolved into it.
> I suddenly realized about six weeks ago that I was managing 30 people.

You may *tumble*, *drift* or *evolve* into management, but you rarely, it seems, *plan* to be there. Perhaps such a feckless approach to life is an artifact of this particular group of managers, but here is a planning manager from New Zealand who, rather to her surprise, has failed to extend her planning skills to the rest of her life:

> – So how did you come to live in Christchurch? [She came from the UK originally.]
> I was sort of drifting around the world and I met someone and I've stayed ever since.
> – Then you didn't plan to be living here?
> It's funny, but I don't apply those principles to my life.

People in fact regularly plan in everyday life: they plan holidays, shopping expeditions, renovations, conception of children, superannuation, and so on. Why, then, does the suggestion that formal planning skills be applied to life as a whole evoke such surprise?[2] How can planning be both helpful and inimical, essential and 'shit', organizing and disorganizing?

Making Lists

To make sense of this ambivalence around planning, it will be helpful to look at the simplest form of plan, the list. Making lists is such a commonplace activity that it has escaped sociological attention, yet, as with Simmel's door, we can sometimes find the profound hiding itself in the obvious.

Managers are often writing lists and these lists evoke far less ambivalence than plans. This manager, for instance, gets more satisfaction from lists than she thinks perhaps she should, so she jokes about it being an obsession:

> – Do you make lists?
> Yeah, yeah, because I'm a Capricorn. It's compulsive. Everyone tells me I'm really organized. I'm always making lists. I have computerized lists that go in my filofax of what I have to do. Then I have another system as part of the diary. At the end of one week, anything that hasn't been done will carry over to the next week. Then I have a master list to stream everything. I know I'm obsessive and I get teased about it a lot.

Lists are a sign of her management. They tell other people that she's 'really organized'. They help control time, creating continuity – 'anything that hasn't been done will carry over to the next week' – but also marking divisions, with the transfer of items 'at the end of one week'. Lists are also something personal that she makes for herself – '*I'm* always *making* lists'. There is a craft satisfaction here in producing something. This production creates *her* as organized. She speaks of '*my* filofax of what *I have to do*'. Writing lists makes an ordered self.

This production of oneself as ordered through an imaginary management of events is evident in another account:

> – When do you start managing in the day?
> When I'm thinking of lists in bed. The thing about this kind of job is there's so many different things. I'd only have a sense of control from spinning out if I have lists to be ticked off. There's too much to keep in one's head.

She starts being a manager in bed by making lists. Lists establish control of a multiplicity that threatens order, 'spinning out' of control. Making lists extends her body to contain that multiplicity, for which her head alone feels insufficient. That sense of control is reinforced as the lists are 'ticked off' and her own control is made visible to herself. With the help of lists she can deal with multiplicity. Writing lists has embodied her as ordered.

This next manager also talks similarly about the way lists order him:

> – Do you make a lot of lists?
> When I get really busy, yes. I'd always have lists going. I tend to update it when I feel my mind's losing control; there's too much to keep hold of, and I'll sit down and make a list.

Once again, lists are a way of taking control when things seem to be multiplying out of control: 'when I feel my mind's losing control, there's too much to keep hold of'. In that common managerial metaphor of handling, lists allow this manager to keep 'hold of' what threatens to get beyond his reach, outside the scope of his own body. Lists create a moment of stasis or fixity in a world that threatens to endlessly move away. The very act of making lists stills movement. This manager *sits down* to make a list; the previous manager makes lists *in bed*. Writing lists works materially on the body. It re-embodies the writer as ordered.

Ordering the Body

How, then, does writing items on a piece of paper, real or imagined, embody us as ordered? When I worked as a manager I normally started the week, and sometimes the day, with a list, and I want to look in detail at one of my own lists here. But the list I am going to look at was made, as were many, in the course of writing this book, because lists are a form of writing that can, amongst other things, organize us to write.

1. library
2. supervision
3. process/revise Taylor
4. transcribe PK
5. unit costing outline
6. cow herding piece
7. planning outline
8. read written chapters. Put in outline

Figure 5.1 'My List'

This list, as shown in Figure 5.1, was made on a completely new page in a notebook, even though it does not fill the page and there was plenty of space for it on the page before. It was, then, a writing deliberately made on its own space: the blank page itself marked a separation from an outside, and in doing so created everything beyond it as outside. Included in that outside in this case were the disorganized writing on my computer and the flux of thoughts around that writing. Setting myself up in front of a blank page to make a list creates a Cartesian moment in which I as subject, abstracted from the flow of events, place myself in front of a space that separates its contents from the flow of events, making them into objects (De Certeau, 1988: 134).

On the space of this blank page I have represented in writing a number of tasks to be undertaken or, more accurately, I have created events as tasks by representing them in this way. These items have not merely been transcribed from memory as they occurred, but are subjected to an arrangement, a *spatial* representation of events that will happen in *time*. The separate items, one below the other, are also a chronology, one that is reinforced by the numbering that accompanies them. This spatial arrangement of time allows the flow of time to be *visible*, to be seen laid out in the present by a self that observes it.

Because the items are discrete and do not merge into one another, they can be attended to separately. This means that their ordering can be rearranged. It also means that the expanse of time in front of me does not have to be engaged all at once. It is divided into separate parts, the crossing of each of which will bring me to the next part, and so on, until the whole space is traversed. The multiplicity of actions is not just fragmentary, but additive, so I am not just 'spinning out', but going in a direction. Moreover, the parts taken separately seem to be within my grasp, even if the whole is not, just as we may feel sometimes that we can get through the next hour, but not through the whole day. The process of ticking off the list can then show me that, if I have not yet grasped the whole, I am moving towards it.

But making the list is not just about making events into tasks. It is also about making me. One feature of this list is particularly revealing: it has never been ticked off. Actually, I think, once it had been made, it was never referred to again, suggesting it was the actual act of making the list itself that had already fulfilled a function. That function is revealed in the unusual neatness and uniformity of the writing when I compare it to other writing in the same notebook. Its order is reinforced by the numbering of each item, something I would normally never do. The numbers are in line, each carefully punctuated with a full stop. The spacing between the numbers and their items is very even. All this suggests an unusual care and deliberation, as if the very act of crafting this list was itself somehow ritually creating someone able to bring about the order that I was seeking. Acting out control in a space that I feel is manageable recreates me as more ordered.

Flow and Space

Writing this list worked because it re-embodied me in a different relation to space and time, so that I experienced myself as more bounded and ordered in relation to a flux of events that seemed to be sweeping me away. Bergson's (1950: 100) distinction between two sorts of time, for which he uses the terms 'time' and 'duration', is helpful in understanding this process. He defines the first type of time, what he calls 'duration', thus:

Pure duration is the form which the succession of our conscious states assumes when our ego lets itself *live*, when it refrains from separating its present state from its former states. For this purpose . . . it is enough that, in recalling those states it does not set them alongside its actual state as one point alongside another, but forms both the past and present states into an organic whole, as happens when we recall the notes of a tune, melting, so to speak, into one another.

Duration, then, is a qualitative organization of conscious states, 'a continuous or qualitative multiplicity with', Bergson adds significantly, 'no resemblance to number' (ibid.: 105). Duration, then, is time as a flow of experience in which events merge into one another. It is not the sort of time that is created by lists.

Bergson's second sort of time, for which he uses the term 'time' itself, is closely bound up with the concept of number. Number, he claims, implies an intuition of space:

> For though we reach a sum by taking into account the succession of different terms, yet it is necessary that each of these terms should remain when we pass to the following, and should wait, so to speak, to be added to the others: ... where could it wait if we did not localise it in space? (ibid.: 79)

We could not count in duration, in which successive qualitative states merge into one another. To count requires a homogeneous medium in which to hold objects simultaneously but separately. This medium is space. Introducing space into our experience of duration:

> ... we set out states of consciousness side by side in such a way as to perceive them simultaneously, no longer in one another, but alongside one another; in a word, we project time into space, we express duration in terms of extensity, and succession in terms of a continuous line or chain, the parts of which touch without penetrating one another. (ibid.: 101)

This suggests how making a list helps us create order. Instead of being swept along by a time in which one state merges into another, it allows us to experience events, like numbers, as a discrete multiplicity, side by side in space, each event waiting to be added to the next. A discrete multiplicity creates singularity. The flow of multiple events becomes separate items. These items can be dealt with one at a time, without worrying how one event merges into the next. They can also be dealt with in a different order, because their visible spatialization allows us to imagine different arrangements, just as we can rearrange a list of numbers.

The space Bergson is talking about is a homogeneous and continuous medium devoid of quality. It is space experienced as separated from duration – the space of Euclidean geometry – a space both empty, but given shape by geometric forms. The list, for example, relies on the concept of a line that gives the individual items direction and cohesion, and of points that fix locations along the line where the items can be placed separately. The points also divide the line so the completion of each individual point – ticking it off – can be imagined as adding up to the complete line. Transposing the flow of time to a finite list of points makes that flow finite, additive, and so manageable.

The Space of Plans

Geometric arrangements in space are so common in management that they often provide a fundamental metaphor for organization itself. The familiar organizational chart is one example. The chart visually presents a collection of people who interact in a flow of time as a geometrical layout within a circumscribed space. Plans also typically depict a development in time as a geometric space. Here, as shown in Figure 5.2, is a plan for a heart health programme (Hawe, Degling and Hall, 1990).

This plan is really a series of nested lists, so that one list 'adds up' to the next list and so on until the goal is reached. The goal is a specific point in future time, although actually depicted as present in space at the same time as everything else on the page. The future is mastered by showing it to be a logical development of the present. The plan allows the time between the 'future' goal and the present to be divided spatially into a series of 'steps' which, as they are completed, accumulate toward the goal. This depiction, moreover, allows for a division of labour, whereby people working on different 'steps' are contributing to the goal without having to concern themselves with the other steps.

A plan such as this allows a complex task to seem achievable. By depicting what has to be done in what order, it shows us, like the list, that the whole task does not need to be approached all at once. Small parts of the task may be experienced as doable, whereas the whole may seem overwhelming, stretching away beyond our grasp. It also makes people's activity visible to themselves and others, as ticks on a list indicate progress. 'You have to have it on paper to show people what you've done', was the way one manager put it.

This additive or cumulative aspect of planning suggests why quantification is so important in management. For example, the objective of the heart health plan is stated as:

To reduce saturated fat intake by 8 per cent amongst men aged between 45 and 64 years in western Sydney by 1993.

As we saw from Bergson's account, this sort of quantification is another application of spatialization. I am no mathematician, and I understand there may be other ways of imagining number than as a spatialized multiplicity, but this latter understanding is certainly the predominant one in management. Time is imagined as a set of arbitrary, equal spaces, ending at the point called 1993.[3] This establishes a definite 'distance' to cross in addressing the problem, which no longer stretches away to infinity. Over this space saturated fat is represented by 100 equivalent points, and of these, 8 must be removed when the space to 1993 is traversed. This not only gives a sense of the dimensions of the task, but also lets us know, each year, if the space is being traversed at the desired pace. Spatializing converts the flow of activity into progress.

```
┌─────────────────────────────────────────────┐
│                     Goal                      │
│   To lower serum cholesterol in men aged      │
│   between 45 and 64 years by 0.5 mmol/L in    │
│        western Sydney by June 1995            │
└─────────────────────────────────────────────┘
```

```
┌─────────────────────────────────────────────┐
│                  Objective                    │
│   To reduce saturated fat intake by 8 per cent│
│   amongst men aged between 45 and 64          │
│          years in western Sydney by 1993      │
└─────────────────────────────────────────────┘
```

Sub-Objectives

- increase knowledge of relationship between dietary fat and serum cholesterol and its importance in reducing cardiovascular disease by 50 per cent by end of the programme
- increase the proportion of healthy food choices at take-away food outlets by 20 per cent within 6 months of beginning of programme
- increase the proportion of low-fat meals served at home by 25 per cent by the end of the programme
- increase knowledge of food content labels in order to facilitate healthier food selection by 50 per cent by end of the programme
- increase proportion of people who like low-fat/low-cost food by 20 per cent within 1 year of the programme

Strategy Objectives

- establish a heart disease and cholesterol risk factor screening, counselling, information and referral service for target group
- train staff in the screening procedure
- provide intensive dietary intervention programmes for those unable to modify own diet
- provide worksite education sessions on heart health for target group
- provide community-based programmes, heart health education programmes including a healthy fast-food choices programme and an education programme on food labelling
- provide low-fat/low-cost cooking programmes for the target group and/or their wives
- increase opportunities for tasting low-fat foods
- contact the managers of fast-food outlets and negotiate the provision of at least one healthy choice
- lobby food standards committee to simplify the labels on food
- train general practitioners in counselling and supporting patients in heart disease prevention

Figure 5.2   *The Plan of a Heart Health Programme (Hawe, Degling, and Hall, 1990)*

Lists versus Plans

So far plans seem to share many of the features of lists, so why the managerial ambivalence? Returning to my own list, a key feature that differentiates it from the heart health plan is that the whole picture is never stated. The list never quite turns into a plan. There is always the implication that there is more to the picture than what is on the list. What it adds up to is left to the imagination, with the possibility that there is something involved beyond the sum of the list, or perhaps the doubt that the list does not really add up to anything. The list does not even have complete sentences. Its connections are not made explicit. This particular list is not necessarily finished. The rest of the page, still waiting to be filled, gives it an extemporized, *ad hoc* character that doesn't require a complete commitment. It can be changed at any time, or thrown away, or replaced by another list. While the list seems to organize an external world, it still connects to me and requires me to make it meaningful. It is very much *my* list. It is a space in relation to me, not something separate. Its setting as space is myself as flow. Hence, by writing it, I relate flow and space within myself.

The heart health plan, however, not only represents Bergson's duration as a series of objects in space, but itself moves closer to being an object. It sets itself apart from my particular experience. Unlike my list, the plan explicitly states the objective towards which the various items are accumulating. It is a self-contained presentation of space. The purpose of the plan is taken out of subjectivity: it is an *objective*. Moreover this purpose is represented as the objective not of a person or persons, but of the plan itself. Its setting as space is the space of its goal. It comes to me already circumscribed.

Stating an objective at once creates the plan as more public.[4] Reconstructing events in the homogeneous space of the plan creates a common space. Any observer can see what the plan is adding up to. This common space is created, however, by imagining it as removed from subjectivity. Objects removed from their part in *my* qualitative experience are also removed from the qualitative experience of *others*. They are thus, in principle, observable by anyone, devoid as they are of any *particular* experience. However, this property of being observable by anyone can lead to the illusion that these objects or events somehow come that way, that this is their reality. In this object world, as Merleau-Ponty (1964: 162) has pointed out, *my* particular situation is then only a possible source of error. I am therefore forced to remove myself as far as possible in order to establish truth. Truth is not a part of that flow wherein I find myself embodied here and now.

But herein lies the source of ambivalence about planning. If I must constantly imagine myself as outside the order I produce so as to establish its truth, it will never work within me. I will be unable to embody it. I may think the plan represents order, but my body will not be ordered by it.

I may, therefore, experience such a plan as irrelevant – I have no relation to it – or my attempts to conform to it may feel positively disorganizing as I attempt to relate things that my body experiences, as unrelated or related differently. Through a triumph of the will I may still achieve the plan, but only with a continued residue of resistance, the resistance of the flow of myself that does not relate to the space of the plan.

The world, including ourselves, we may say is neither space nor flow, but the one in relation to the other. We live this relation in our bodies. Disorganization is that embodied experience of ourselves dissipating and flowing away from us. Planning can re-embody us as singular and ordered in relation to that flowing away, just as concepts can stabilize the movement of language, bounding it and stilling its combinatory possibilities so that we can return with some confidence to a meaning that has not shifted. But if concepts leave us there with a fixed meaning, we will have a language that is either dead – that we do not relate to – or jarring – disrupting our sense of meaning. Plans also, to be effective, must embody us as closed and singular within a fluid openness of possibility, or they leave us stranded in a disembodiment at odds with the order of duration that we continue to experience around the plans. Planning, to work, must embody us as spatialized within the flow of time. Then we experience it as organizing. Treating spatialization as somehow fundamental, effectively alienates us from our own order. Order becomes a space that traps us and cuts us off from living. Lists are less likely to be alienating in this way because their ad hoc and personal character gives them an inbuilt relation to the differently embodied subjectivity that developed them.[5]

Managed by Objectives

Failure to appreciate the metaphoric nature of planning, to understand that organization is not a literal conformity to the plan's meaning, can easily vitiate attempts to make planning more useful. 'Management by Objectives' (MBO) was a term coined by Peter Drucker in the early 1950s in the context of a critique of Taylor's scientific management. For Drucker (1954), scientific management, by prescribing every detail of the work process, takes the risk and vitality out of management, turning managers into mere administrators – custodians rather than directors of their enterprise. Management, he claims, is a practice, not a science or a profession:

> any serious attempt to make management 'scientific' or a 'profession' is bound to lead to the attempt to eliminate those 'disturbing nuisances', the unpredictabilities of business life . . . and, in the process, the economy's freedom and ability to grow. (1954: 10)

In effect, Drucker wants to open management to duration – to the flow of development through time. Organic images of growth replace the

Relate to Sun

Taylorist emphasis on mechanism. Not only should the economy be an area of freedom and ability 'to grow', but the manager should be 'the dynamic, life-giving element' in every business (ibid.: 3).

MBO tries to integrate vitality and order by prescribing the results or objectives to be achieved, but leaving it up to individual managers as to how best to achieve them. Ideally, there should be a movement between the manager's sense of autonomy and the planned direction of the organization. One advantage of this approach is that it requires less management because everyone is, to some extent, managing themselves, as this manager makes clear:

> To me, management is largely about giving people responsibility, and coming to a contract, that that is their area of responsibility if they are reaching their goals, reaching their objective as set. Otherwise I do not interfere and re-order their priorities.

The end points are set, but managers move through the intervening space in their own way.

The very term 'management by objectives', however, is inherently problematic. 'Objectives' do not, in fact, manage. Constituted as *objective*, they remain apart from us as *subjects*. The illusion that objectives manage contradicts that very 'freedom and ability to grow' that MBO was set up to stimulate. By circumscribing duration from the standpoint of spatial-ized time, one term in the relation is set up as privileged over the other, and metaphoricity fails. What we have is another strategy of admitting metaphoricity on condition that it is contained within a containing, higher realm. Failure to sustain the dynamism of metaphor in these conditions can be seen when MBO is presented as a formalized system by Ordione in the 1960s. Ordione (1965: 60) actually characterizes the desired objective geometrically, as a 'fixed terminal point' around which the entire space of management is then reconstructed.

> Most good work in management aims at accomplishing some specific end – achieving a particular goal, solving a particular problem, or reaching some fixed terminal point. The definition of these objectives for the whole organization, for all its subordinate organizations, and for the individuals in them is the logical starting place for management improvement.

The geometry of the fixed terminal point reaches back to become the logical starting place for management, with its end implied in its beginning. Around this point is organized a hierarchy of goals – for 'the whole organization', for 'subordinate organizations' and for 'the indi-viduals in them'. 'If you don't have a goal,' Ordione claims, 'you have no idea of whether you are on the right road or not' (ibid.: 60). The image of the right road implies a future – the end of the road – already present in the beginning. 'Freedom and ability to grow' however, may require trying a variety of roads, or leaving the road altogether. Ordione's 'right road' presents as an objective the very conformity MBO was set up to avoid. Duration, as the correct way from A to B, is now immobilized. As Peters (1987: 510) comments, '(m)anagement by objectives (MBO) is one more great idea that has been neutered by bureaucrats in nine out of ten applications'. Planning is 'neutered' if it fails to work metaphorically. It fails to embody us as ordered within the flow of possibility, and so becomes barren.

Fixity and Movement

The capacity of planning to embody fixity within movement, to order us within the flow of time, is critical to whether we experience planning as organizing or disorganizing. The following two accounts differ radically about the value of formal planning, but the difference really revolves around that capacity. The first account begins with a common distinction in management between 'policy/planning' and 'operations', to the detriment of the former:

> When I was working in the Health Department I was working in a classic policy/planning role, and I realise how ineffectual as far as achieving a result is concerned a planning and policy role is in the balance between policy and operations – that operations, if effectively managed, is where the control and decision lies . . . When you write papers or guidelines or frameworks or whatever, they never get translated into what you thought it would be.

This manager experiences planning as quite removed from action, and therefore from organization. That 'paper', he complains, never gets 'translated' into 'what you thought it would be'. Translation fails, he goes on to say, because management is characterized by rapid movement:

> I think the successful operational manager is the one who is rapidly assessing and analysing, and rapidly making judgements.

Planning, on the other hand, creates a different mind in a different body:

> It's a different mind and different skill to the capacity to sit down and spend long periods of time writing, analysing. A completely different skill to an operational manager's skill, and rarely do the two come together in the one person.

Planning creates a fixed, not a moving body. The two bodies are incompatible, so much so that contact with what he calls 'the realities' – operations – actually paralyses what little movement there is in policy:

> Basically you can't write policy if you know much about operations . . . If you
> know a lot about the realities you become completely paralysed in a policy
> sense.

Rapidity and stasis: there is no flow between them. Even where the two
bodies are contained in one body, they do not combine; there can only be
a difficult switching from one to the other:

> And . . . doing them both at the same time, it's extremely difficult to flip from
> one role to the other.

Planning does not embody the operational manager as organized. It does
not work metaphorically. Fixity removes this manager from reality, which
is movement.

If this manager moved out of planning in order to manage, the next
thinks that managing in her area of work is impossible without it:

> You have a strategic plan and business plans and annual reports. And
> every programme should have a plan. I'm just completely into that. All that
> architecture and planning, that's just what I bring with me as a style of
> working.

Planning forms her as a manager. It is an 'architecture' that she is 'just
completely into', so much so that it gives her manner of acting in
management, her 'style'. The 'architecture' of planning works to embody
her as organized. Its space, like Simmel's hut, creates her as ordered in
relation to the multiplicity of possibilities outside it.

Planning, in our previous manager's account, immobilizes, whereas for
this manager, it make movement possible. To explain this she uses
another metaphor of spatiality, the map:

> One of the strategic plans we've made is a nutrition plan, and it sort of maps out
> the way that we thought ahead that we'd cover. And WP [the nutritionist]
> works her way through that. What exactly she works on in any one year is
> opportunistic. Like we might put something on hold until next year, but the
> plan maps it out. It's a reference point, and she uses it really well. But that
> doesn't mean it controls you, or you can't change things. I think it's a really
> good plan. I get involved in that. I like how she uses it. It's incredibly helpful.

Planning here is a map that represents as present in space 'the way we
thought ahead' in time. 'WP works her way through that', – it sets her
moving, translating space back into time again. Mapping in this way
allows movement around time. Something can be put 'on hold' this year,
and will still be there next year. Events this way can be grasped, held. By
providing a 'reference point', movement in time becomes a journey rather
than just wandering. But it is a journey, not a stasis, so the plan does not
feel like a trap. Rather than serving the plan, she feels it re-creates her

bodily as organized: it creates an 'I' that can 'get involved' rather than remain at a distance. The plan moves her pleasurably: she 'like(s)' how WP uses it. So it can be 'incredibly helpful'. Planning here works metaphorically and does not leave its users outside their own organization. It creates an embodied organization, not a body at odds with its organization. In the case of our previous manager, writing the plan is actually disorganizing; here it is organizing.

Fixity or Movement?

Because spatialization – Bergson's 'time' – has been so traditionally enmeshed in thinking about management and organization there has been, in recent postmodern writing, a tendency to privilege metaphors of flow and change over those of space and stasis.[6]

Change has become a mantra for management gurus like Peters (1992: 378): 'Everything is in flux. Everything *is* flux' – while more sophisticated statements like those of Chia (1996: 117) have essentially the same emphasis:

> The postmodern style of thinking is one which privileges an ontology of movement, emergence and becoming whereby the transient and ephemeral nature of what is 'real' is accentuated.

By adopting an ontology of stasis, organization studies, and indeed Western thought in general, Chia argues, attempts to control this flow by representing it as fixity, seducing us ' into thinking about organizations as free-standing entities rather than as effects produced through precariously balanced figurational patterns of actions and interactions' (ibid.: 1996, 143).

This postmodern privileging of flux is prefigured in Bergson himself. His concern to rescue duration from time often gives the impression of rescuing life from death:

> [S]ensations and tastes seem to me to be *objects* as soon as I isolate and name them, and in the human soul there are only processes (1950: 131).

Language – the process of naming – turns things into objects and so places them outside the soul, which only lives in duration. For Bergson in this vein, spatialization defeats process by turning duration into time.[7]

Elsewhere, however, Bergson is less dualistic about his time/duration distinction in a way that is, I think, more helpful for our argument. Multiplicity itself, he states, whether in its discrete form as time or its merged form as duration, only exists for consciousness. It is not some primary form of being, because our experience of being is never primary. It is a product of interaction between ourselves and the world: 'Each of the so-called successive states of the external world exists alone: their multiplicity is real only for a consciousness that can first retain them and then set them side by side by externalizing them in relation to one another' (ibid.: 120). Each of the two states of time, then, is a *product* of consciousness as it either retains, or sets side by side, successive states of the external world. Time and duration can in fact be seen as mutually dependent, the one always creating the other for us as the undefined background from which it differentiates itself.[8] We can see this mutual dependence more clearly in revisiting Bergson's definition of 'duration' given earlier:

> Pure duration is the form which the succession of our conscious states assumes when our ego lets itself *live*, when it refrains from separating its present state from its former states. For this purpose it need not be entirely absorbed in the passing sensation or idea; for then, on the contrary, it would no longer *endure*. Nor need it forget its former states: it is enough that, in recalling those states it does not set them alongside its actual state as one point alongside another, but forms both the past and present states into an organic whole, as happens when we recall the notes of a tune, melting, so to speak, into one another (ibid.: 100).

As he points out, if we were entirely absorbed in passing sensations or ideas, they would not *endure* – there would be no duration. But how could we conceive ourselves as not absorbed in the flow of events unless we could somehow project ourselves as *outside* them – as a consciousness that 'refrains from separating its present state from its former states', but allows them to melt into an organic whole? But the very movement of getting *outside* the *flow* requires a relation between space and flow. A sense of 'duration' creates our sense of 'time', and vice versa, because our bodies – Bergson would say consciousness – can only experience relationally.[9] To simply substitute flow for stasis, 'duration' for 'time', creates an unchanging change that, as Game (1997) has pointed out, itself feels curiously static.

The ability to externalize events from one another in lists and plans, to imagine their 'radical distinctness', to have them waiting in space where we left them while we examine different events, to imagine ourselves as somehow outside this space, all these ordering activities create a sense of organization and control. Coming from a duration that seems to be 'spinning out', dissipating us with it, imagining events as spatialized re-embodies us as organized. It can only do this, however, if there is a relation between space and flow, and if that relation can be embodied as experience. Otherwise space and flow produce incompatible embodiments, and our ordering disorganizes us.

However, if flow and space depend on one another, it follows that the embodiment of ourselves as organized might require a movement in either direction. This possibility is implicit in the paradoxical attitude to planning that we reviewed at the beginning of the chapter. Experiencing the world as a discrete multiplicity may leave us disconnected, fragmented, lifeless. Re-embodying a sense of organization will not be achieved by a further movement into spatialized time, but will more likely require a movement back towards the continuous multiplicity of duration. This latter sense of organization is beautifully expressed by Wallace Stevens, whose combination of the careers of poet and manager should remind us that there are other sorts of writing than plans and lists, and that this other writing can also organize us, but quite differently. In a letter to his wife, Stevens wrote:

> Sometimes I am terribly jangled, full of clashing things. But always the first harmony comes from something I cannot just say to you at the moment – the touch of you organizing me again. (quoted in Richardson, 1986: 332)

I can immediately respond to this, but am also constantly surprised by that juxtaposition of touch and organization. The surprise comes, I think, because our sense of organization is so formed by the order of spatialization, with its dependence on vision, on *seeing* things as an arrangement in space. Touch, as evoked here, seems the very antithesis of this. In Stevens' expression, it reconnects a you and a me. He experiences himself not as disconnected and separate, but as related to another person, who takes him beyond his isolated self and reconnects him to his own organization.

Order as Metaphoric

I began by asking how order could be thought in the context of metaphor, but outside a relation of control. Simmel's image of the door once again comes to our aid. If between the orders of spatialized time and duration there is a door that opens and shuts, time and duration are no longer in opposition, but are always experienced as potentially or actually in relation. Planning may momentarily shut the door on a flow of events that seems bewildering and disorienting, in which we feel ourselves dissipating. It then re-embodies us as whole and ordered in relation to that flow, allowing us to re-enter it meaningfully. Planning in this case works metaphorically to organize us. But if it is a locking of the door, we will feel cut off from that possibility that our body still dimly experiences. We may feel that planning has somehow put us in the wrong body – still, when we feel moving; or we may no longer feel 'on the pulse', but instead forced 'to give up those [things] that [we've] got organized'. Our order will disorganize us. Order, then, is not something we can achieve absolutely. It is not the end point of managing; if it is to organize us, it must itself be managed, which is to say it must work metaphorically.

Notes

1 A range of responses also reflected in Marshall and Stewart, 1981.

2 As a manager I frequently received promotional material for seminars and publications encouraging me to do just that – to plan my entire life. For example, one course, 'Tactics for Winning', claims to be a personal effectiveness programme to enhance my potential in the areas of career, social interaction, and personal life. To do this effectively it seems you must:

- identify appropriate goals and formulate them
- develop a plan to effect these goals
- create a system for monitoring your own progress
- identify personality and character flaws that might impede your goal achievement
- design a self-development programme to overcome the above impediments
- do effective daily, weekly, and long-term time-management planning.

3 In the same way, of course, men, who are living in duration, are imagined as crossing a series of equal, arbitrary points, and the ones between the 45th point and the 64th point are selected from all the others as the object of the programme.

4 This public and impersonal character is implicit in the spatialization of time itself, as Durkheim (1965: 23) makes clear in terms akin to Bergson's:

[Time] is an abstract and impersonal frame which surrounds not only our individual existence, but that of all humanity. It is like an endless chart, where all duration is spread out before the mind, and upon which all possible events can be located in relation to fixed and determined guidelines. It is not *my time* that is thus arranged; it is time in general such as it is objectively thought of by everybody in a single civilisation.

5 Arnold Lobel's (1992) story, 'A List', however, gives a delightful account of being trapped in the space of the list. One morning in bed Toad decides to make a list to organize his day. It contains items such as 'Wake Up', 'Get Dressed', 'Take a Walk with Frog', and so on, which he can cross off as they are completed. On the walk with Frog, however, the list blows away. Toad can't run and catch it because that wasn't an item on his list. He and Frog are forced to sit and do nothing until it gets dark, when Toad remembers the last item on his list: 'Go to Sleep'. He writes this on the ground with a stick, crosses it out, and they both fall asleep.

6 While characterizing the tendency as 'postmodern' it can also be seen as developing from the reaction to the role of rational control in organization brought about by empirical studies in the 1970s, findings summarized thus by Stewart (1983: 96–7):

The picture that emerges from studies of what managers do is of someone who lives in a whirl of activity, in which attention must be switched every few minutes from one subject, problem, and person to another, of an uncertain world where relevant information includes gossip and speculation about how other people are thinking and what they are likely to do . . . In short, it is a much more human activity than that commonly suggested in management textbooks.

7 Gurvitch (1990) notes that both Bachelard and Piaget expressed surprise at Bergson's contention that he had nothing to learn from Einstein, given the latter's profound interest in the relation of space and time. Gurvitch himself concludes that Bergson 'lacked the dialectical frame of mind' (ibid.: 39).

8 Metzner (1994) points out that historically there have been two main metaphors for consciousness, one spatial or topographical, and the other temporal or biographical.

9 Loy (1988: 217) expresses the antithesis thus:

Consider a solitary rock out of an ocean current, protruding above the surface. Whether one is on the rock or floating past it, it is the relation between the two that makes both movement and rest possible.

6

MANAGING AND DISORDER

It might seem surprising to discover that order requires managing if it is to organize us, but the assertion that disorder also requires managing comes as no surprise. Managing often seems to be largely about keeping disorder at bay, and that is true not only for professional managers, but also for our more everyday managing selves. When asked how we are after a stressful or difficult time and we reply that we're 'managing', or even 'just managing', we imply that something survives amid the mess and disorder that assails us, and that our separation from that mess confirms that we are still there, if only barely. In a negative way, we affirm ourselves; something survives separate from disorder. This separation, affirming as it does that 'X' (order) is not, in fact, 'not-X' (disorder), appears at first glance, to be the very reverse of the metaphoricity involved in effective managing. But we shall see that this process of separation only works if it too works metaphorically, i.e. if it embodies us in relation to disorder. Otherwise the order that remains is not possibility, but merely vacancy.

Putting Out the Rubbish

'Just managing' is a minimalist sort of managing, but separating ourselves from rubbish can be a more positive experience. Italo Calvino (1993: 102) has written evocatively about his daily ritual of putting out the rubbish, and its place in managing, not just garbage, but himself:

> the ... unwritten law to which the ritual of our daily habits bows dictates that expulsion of the day's rubbish coincide with the winding up of the same day, and that one can go to sleep after having removed from the house any possible sources of unpleasant smells ... not just out of a natural concern for hygiene but so that on waking up the following morning one may begin the new day without having to touch what the evening before we cast off from ourselves forever.

Putting out the rubbish, while closing the day, is also a gesture of promise. A new day will be possible because there is something to start with. It is a gesture that confirms the self:

the gesture of throwing away is the first and indispensable condition of being, since one is what one does not throw away (ibid.: 104)

Clearing away confirms a whole and clean self with no clinging, unpleasant smells or touch of corruption. Our boundaries are clear, with ourselves on one side, and what we have discarded on the other. But this closure that is marked by putting out the rubbish is also an opening; it is an opening to a new day, to the promise of possibility. It is an emptiness, certainly, but one that is available for new relations. Bachelard (1969: xxviii–ix) speaks of a necessary vacancy that makes creation possible:

> Knowing must therefore be accompanied by an equal capacity to forget knowing. Not-knowing is not a form of ignorance but a difficult transcendence of knowledge. This is the price that must be paid for an oeuvre to be, at all times, a sort of pure beginning, which makes its creation an exercise in freedom.[1]

We must, Bachelard suggests, make a break with the accumulation of the past, be it knowing, memory, or bad smells, otherwise there will be no possibility of the new. Putting out the rubbish is a necessary moment in managing ourselves. But this self, in the case of both Calvino and Bachelard, is not just vacancy. It is a vacancy in relation to what it might become. It is a metaphoric opening to possibility.[2] But what are the conditions of this sort of vacancy and how does it relate to the rubbish that has been put aside? Let us approach this question by way of management's desire for cleanliness.

A Clean Sheet of Paper

That daily renewal described by Calvino for the individual is prescribed by Peters for the organization. 'Tomorrow's effective "organization"', he proclaims, 'will be conjured up anew each day' (1992: 11). But to begin anew the old must be thrust away, the rubbish from the previous day put out. This fantasy of beginning again with a clean break from the past has, paradoxically, become something of a management tradition. I received the following example from Qantas Airlines while working on this chapter:

> Dear Mr Lennie,
> August marks the beginning of a new era for Qantas. We are introducing the most significant overhaul of our products and services since the introduction of the Boeing 747 aircraft in the early 1970s.
> Following a programme of seeking and receiving customer comments, we are in the process of redesigning almost every aspect of our operations. You will begin to see changes on the ground and in the air from early next month.

The letter goes on to highlight some of these changes: 'a whole new cabin interior with a distinct Australian theme', 'new uniforms for ground crew

and cabin staff', 'lighter and healthier meals', 'new amenities kits' – all
something of an anti-climax after that promise of 'the beginning of a new
era' but the appeal to a desire to start again is clear enough.

In a book whose title links today's 'revolutionary' management with its
engineering past, *Re-engineering the Corporation: A Manifesto for Business
Revolution*, Hammer and Champy (1993) propose a ritual suspension of
established company assumptions, to allow space for new processes and
procedures to develop. In terms that recall Henry Ford's 'history is bunk',
they emphasize the absolute break with the past: 'Tradition counts for
nothing. Re-engineering is a new beginning' (ibid.: 49).

To evoke that sense of beginning again, Hammer and Champy appeal
to the figure of the writer:

> For a writer, nothing is so exciting and at the same time so terrifying, as a clean
> sheet of paper or a blank computer screen. (ibid.: 134)

Re-engineering the company is made possible through a ritual removal
of the rubbish of the past, a renewal that metaphorically re-embodies the
manager as a writer, with the clean sheet of paper as the promise of 'a
pure beginning'. But Bachelard speaks of 'a difficult transcendence of
knowledge' and 'a price that must be paid' to reach that pure beginning.
We may feel that Hammer and Champy, particularly following the Qantas
example, arrive at their pure beginning a little too easily, which is why the
results of the process often seem to be trivial.

That work of separation from rubbish paradoxically requires involvement with it, an involvement that not only professional management
would wish to deny. We can see this denial in the very fantasy of the
writer in front of a clean sheet of paper, because, as Gallop (1988) has
reminded us, the fantasy encourages us to repress the very work of
managing that allows its possibility. Discussing a collection of essays on
women's writing, one of which includes a meditation on a well known
depiction of writing by Vermeer: 'Lady Writing a Letter and Her Maid
Servant', Gallop comments:

> There is a class of women who write and a class who serve those who write.
> Leclerc writes [about Vermeer's painting]: 'Admit finally that there is in this
> woman writing, a spoiled woman (*femme gâtée*) . . . a woman for whom the quill
> came into her fingers without her having to pluck it from the bird's wing' (pp.
> 138–9). Writing is not just a work of the spirit; there are material requisites, labor
> must be done by another so that this woman can write. (1988: 167)

Something of this relation still holds to-day, Gallop claims. There are
'women of another class whose labor we rely on so that we can write: the
women who clean our houses, care for our children, type our manu-
scripts; cleaning women and secretaries, for example' (ibid.: 169). But
while Vermeer's picture makes this subordination clear, it vanishes in our
fantasy of the writer in front of a clean sheet of paper. Gallop recalls how

the very dust jacket of the book she was discussing made this clear. She had been working with a library copy, but was later given a new book. On the dust jacket was Vermeer's painting reproduced – but with the maidservant deleted. In order to depict the freedom of a woman writing alone at her table, the woman she depended on had been, literally, effaced.

Housekeeping

That effacement of the maidservant recalls another derivation of the term 'management'. We have already mentioned one derivation, from the Italian *maneggiare*, to handle or train horses. That meaning, with its implications of domination and control, is the established one in professional management. However, Williams (1983: 190) gives another:

> Its subsequent history is affected by confusion with *ménager*, French – to use carefully, from *ménage* – household, which goes back to *mansionaticum*, vulgar Latin and root word of *mansioneum*, Latin – a dwelling (which led directly to *maison*, French – house). There is ample evidence from late C17 and C19 of overlap between *manage* and *menage*, expressed in variations of spelling. This affected the senses of *manager*, from trainer and director (*maneggiare*) to careful housekeeper (*ménager*). This range is still active in the language, with applications from sport to business to housekeeping (a good manager).

Housekeeping for me evokes Simmel's image once again, of the hut separated from the infinity of space, and the labour required to maintain that separation. Here is a space where we work to separate ourselves from disorder so we are ready to step out into possibility – a significant moment in managing. Housekeeping, however, is a decidedly subordinated moment in professional management, which separates itself from dealing with rubbish and disorder as far as possible, delegating the task to people whose status, remuneration and (sometimes) gender mark them as subordinate. A frequent sign of status in management is to have one's own secretary to deal with all the bits and pieces, contact with which might signify the manager as merely a housekeeper. In her study of secretaries, Pringle (1988: 1, 2) points out that the only effective definition of 'secretary' is 'not a boss', and remarks that it 'is one of the few employment categories for which there has never been a clear job description'. The very definition of this category is itself messy, the reversal of the order and clarity that goes, in fantasy at least, with being the boss. Yet if the boss is called the manager, the secretary is essential to their management.

As a manager I never had a personal secretary, but the same separation and subordination of people who deal with the materiality of trivia, bits and pieces, dirt and disorder, still applied in my office. I wrote my memos and reports on clean sheets of paper, but the secretaries did the word processing and filing, took most phone calls, booked travel, ordered clean sheets of paper, pens and general stationery, and organized to have the computer serviced and repaired. They dealt with all the bits and pieces. They also dealt with anyone who came in the door. They screened me from unwanted calls, both official and personal: 'Mr Lennie is with a client; is in conference; is tied up; has just stepped out.' While not being my personal secretary, any secretary 'knew' to give my work priority, though there was no official policy on this. I cannot say I did much to discourage the custom. There was also a cleaner whom I rarely even saw. He was on contract and came in on weekends.

   In order, then, that I as a manager could 'write', a whole organization of filtering, filing, cleaning, maintenance, and replacement had to come about. The subordination of all this housekeeping was marked by gender, by remuneration, and by status. There was an office manager and two secretaries – all female. The secretaries were paid a little over a third of what I received. The cleaner, the one most directly handling dirt and garbage, was male, but a student on contract, not a fulltime worker. He was 'handled' by the office manager, but was not considered directly part of the staff. So it was not just myself managing this office, but a group of people linked in a way that meant that I did not have to recognize my managing in them, and hence my connection with the disorder that they handled. I could indulge, up to a point, through a structure that allowed me to forget my relation to it, a sense that I had no part in that disorder.

   Most managers do recognize some housekeeping aspects of their work, but with considerable impatience. It is usually experienced as distraction from the 'real job':

> Although I accept in management it's like this, that I'm being held up from what I'm meant to be doing . . . the trouble is you never get to that stage when it is really a clean desk, you really have done whatever it is you need to be doing.

This manager fears she may never become that writer in front of a clean sheet of paper, giving rise to the suspicion that she might really be only the housekeeper. Another manager feels overwhelmed by trivia, and feels this positions her literally as a household manager:

> – What don't you like about management?
>   There are a lot of areas I don't like. I hate the administrivia as I call it. I hate it. I just loathe all that!
> – I can see six in-trays piled up there.
>   Yeah, they're the last things I want to deal with. I feel overwhelmed by it.
> – Anything else?
>   Oh, this is a kindergarten. You're trying to get away from 'I'm not your mother'. I've had some gross problems with staff expectations. Anything that goes wrong, you fix it!

Details of administration and demanding staff are always there cluttering up the clean space of management, reminding her that she is still a housekeeper and mother when she comes to work.[3]

Next to Godliness

Despite the subordination of housekeeping, we have also remarked that *The Book of Household Management* by Mrs Isabella Beeton (1861) was probably the most successful book on management ever written. But what can a book about an activity that most managers think they should have left behind when they start the business of managing, tell us about our topic? Not very much if management literature is anything to go by. I have only been able to find one article (Wensley, 1996) taking Mrs Beeton seriously as a manager. However, I suggest that the subordination of domesticity to management 'proper' is another manifestation of disembodiment, of a refusal to recognize the metaphoric nature of managing. It is possible, then, that a text on the activity that has been 'left behind' can tell us more about managing in a more embodied way than many 'proper' management texts. That being said, we have to read Mrs Beeton with care because in her zeal to have household management taken seriously, she often presents it as a strategy of disembodied control.

Cleaning is something Mrs Beeton takes very seriously. 'Cleanliness', she states, 'is next to godliness . . . and order is in the next degree' (1861: 998). So the manager, who is the mistress of the house, begins her day with a ritual that relates cleaning her body to an order beyond it, cleaning the house:

> Cleanliness . . . must be studied both in regard to the person and the house, and all that it contains. Cold or tepid baths should be employed every morning, unless, on account of illness or other circumstances, they should be deemed objectionable. (ibid.: 2)

Here Mrs Beeton identifies a relation between 'the person' and 'the house' and 'all it contains'. It is this relation between cleaning herself and cleaning what is around her that creates the life, or spirit, of the household. That spirit is a social hierarchy that culminates in, and is unified by, the mistress herself. Describing 'THE MISTRESS' Mrs Beeton says:

> As with the commander of an army, or the leader of any enterprise, so it is with the mistress of a house. Her spirit will be seen through the whole establishment; and just in proportion as she performs her duties intelligently and thoroughly, so will her domestics follow in her path. (ibid.: 1)

The mistress' cleaning of her person signals the beginning of a meticulous routine of cleaning, dusting, scrubbing, and polishing that lasts the whole day. Mrs Beeton engages in immense detail with the materiality of cleaning, only some of which we shall follow here to give a feel for the process.

Starting at six o'clock in summer and 6.30 in winter, the housemaid is to begin by taking up the hearth-rugs in the breakfast room and sweeping the room. Placing her housemaid's box in front of the stove:

> She now sweeps up the ashes, and deposits them in her cinder-pail, which is a japanned tin pail, with a wire-sifter inside, and a closely-fitting top. In this pail the cinders are sifted, and reserved for use in the kitchen or under the copper, the ashes only being thrown away. The cinders disposed of, she proceeds to black-lead the grate, producing the black lead, the soft brush for laying it on, her blacking and polishing brushes, from the box which contains her tools. (ibid.: 988–9)

Having polished the grates and lighted all necessary fires:

> the housemaid proceeds with her dusting, and polishing the several pieces of furniture in the breakfast parlour, leaving no corner unvisited. (ibid.: 991)

The dining room requires even more care than the other rooms, and the glassware and plate must be polished, the latter standing for good management of the entire household:

> Few things add more to the neat and comfortable appearance of a dinner-table than well-polished plate; indeed, the state of the plate is a certain indication of a well-managed or ill-managed household. (ibid.: 995)

The cleaning routine continues thus through all the rooms of the house and throughout the day, only ceasing after tea when the housemaid assists her mistress 'to undress then put her dress in order for the morrow', and 'the fire is made up for the night, fireguard replaced, and everything in the room left in order for the night' (ibid.: 997). The mistress and the house are then left ready to begin a new day.

Through this cleaning ritual that flows from the mistress' cleaning of herself the entire physical surface of the house is cleaned each day 'leaving no corner unvisited'; but this removal of the accumulation of the day before also helps to embody it as a household. Bachelard (1969: 68) evokes this creative aspect of housework when he writes:

> The housewife awakens furniture that was asleep. . . . A house that shines from the care it receives appears to have been rebuilt from the inside; it is as though it were new inside.

The housewife who must awaken the often reluctant furniture every day may well feel less rapturous. Nevertheless, Bachelard here counters that tendency to depict cleaning only as drudgery. Rather, he is saying, it can be about creating the same possibilities for renewal of our life as Calvino's putting out the rubbish. It is the 'gesture of throwing away' that affirms being. 'What a great life it would be' Bachelard exclaims, 'if, every morning, every object in the house could be made anew by our hands, could 'issue' from our hands' (ibid.: 69).

The household is awakened when cleaning works metaphorically: it becomes not just a vacant collection of objects, but an embodied relation between the self and its environment, a relation that creates us as ready for living. Through the cleaning routine, moreover, inert space – Bergson's 'time' – opens up to duration. The day is created as time in which the household can live, just as Calvino's putting out the rubbish creates for him the new day as possibility, not just another empty space to be filled. This is perhaps why cleanliness might be experienced as 'next to godliness.'

Recognizing Rubbish

But if the creation of ourselves as clean and ordered requires separation from disorder, how do we recognize the latter? When Calvino affirms himself by putting out the rubbish, how does he know what is rubbish and what is not? This seemingly simple issue turns out to be quite complex.

The separation from rubbish as a guarantee of integrity, of a whole and clean self, is the theme of the Biblical book of Leviticus and its myriad, puzzling prohibitions:

> I am the Lord your God, who have separated you from the peoples. You shall therefore make a distinction between the clean beast and the unclean, and between the unclean bird and the clean; you shall not make yourselves abominable by beast or by bird or by anything with which the ground teems, which I have set apart for you to hold unclean. You shall be holy to me; for I the Lord am holy, and have separated you from the peoples, that you should be mine. (Lev. 20.24–6)

The long list of unclean beasts, birds, and other abominations that follows looks, on the face of it, completely arbitrary. Mary Douglas (1966) has argued, however, that these 'abominations of Leviticus' are neither arbitrary commands to test obedience to God nor an early version of rules for public hygiene, but the by-product of a system of ordering. Her argument leads to some fertile speculation about ordering in general and its relationship to rubbish, dirt, and disorder.

For Douglas (ibid.: 53), what is prohibited is anything that undermines or threatens orderly classification. As holiness requires that different classes of things shall not be confused, prohibited animals are those that belong to confused classes: sea creatures that have neither fins nor scales, as these partake of both land and sea; winged creatures that go on all fours, as these partake of air and land; creatures that swarm on the earth, neither walking nor flying. Animals that part the hoof and chew the cud are clean, but the rock badger is unclean 'because it chews the cud but does not part the hoof' (Lev. 11.5), as is the swine 'because it parts the hoof and is cloven-footed but does not chew the cud' (Lev. 11.7). Bodily fluids – blood, semen, etc. – are unclean because they cross the boundary between the body and the outside world, threatening the body's integrity. What is clearly separate from us is not threatening to us. It does not undermine our order. The threat comes from what might blur clarity, endangering that separateness and the boundaries of ourselves.

Douglas argues that the unclean – dirt – is essentially dis*order*, and that the reaction to dirt is continuous with other reactions to ambiguity or anomaly (1966: 4, 5). Dirt threatens integrity and order, making boundaries unclear and breaking down classification. Dirt, Douglas claims (ibid.: 35), in a phrase borrowed from William James, is 'matter out of place'. It follows that:

> Dirt is never a unique, isolated event. Where there is dirt there is system. Dirt is the by-product of a systematic ordering and classification of matter (ibid.: 35).

Order and dirt are antithetical certainly, but they also depend on one another. They only exist relationally. What is bounded and whole exists only in relation to what is unbounded and dissipated, to what threatens to leak across or invade boundaries, breaking down clarity and integrity. Management abounds with examples of this.

A By-product of Order

In Mrs Beeton's household we find that housekeeping is inserted in a hierarchy that ranges from, at the lowest, servants brought in from outside, to, at the summit, the mistress of the house. As this hierarchy represents an increasing social distance of civilization from the dirt and disorder that would threaten it, so its assertion allows the recognition of the form and proximity of disorder.[4] Speaking of that exigency when the mistress might have to call in hired assistance to nurse a sick child, Mrs Beeton (1861: 1025, 6) commiserates:

> she must trust the dearest obligation of her life to one who, from her social sphere, has probably notions of rearing children diametrically opposed to the preconceived ideas of the mother . . . It has been justly said – we think by Hood – that the children of the poor are not brought up, *but dragged up* . . . and that children, reared in the reeking dens of squalor and poverty, live at all, is an apparent anomaly in the course of things, that, at first sight, would seem to set the laws of sanitary provision at defiance.

The poor inhabit a nether-world between civilization and nature. They blur the clarity of what it is to be civilized. Their children are *dragged* up, neither erect nor on the ground. They live, not in houses, but in *dens*, and they do not smell human, they *reek*, seeping offensively into the very body of civilization through its nostrils.

Servants from outside the household are recognized as particularly dangerous because they come from direct contact with the source of dirt and disorder itself. But servants generally, however indispensable, always signal the threat of their possibly ambiguous social origins, a threat whose ubiquity Mrs Beeton here satirizes:

> It is the custom of 'Society' to abuse its servants – a *façon de parler*, such as leads their lords and masters to talk of the weather, and, when rurally inclined of the crops, – leads matronly ladies, and ladies just entering on their probation in that borrowed and honourable state, to talk of servants, and as we are told, wax eloquent over the greatest plague in life while taking a quiet cup of tea. (ibid.: 961)

'The weather', 'the crops', 'plague': it is nature that constantly makes itself present, smearing, scratching, rusting the polished surface of society; and the servants, while engaged on the side of order, are also prone to partaking of disorder. Their ubiquitous presence ensures that the dirt and disorder into which their class reaches is never entirely forgotten. They move between the household and what it would exclude, threatening distinctions. Ideally, therefore, they should be present but not visible or audible, their bodies inhabiting a different space:

> the footman should tread lightly in moving around, and, if possible, should bear in mind, if there is a wit or humourist of the party, whose good things keep the table in a roar, that they are not expected to reach his ears. (Beeton, 1861: 968)

> Attendants in the drawing room, even more than in the dining-room, should move about actively but noiselessly; no creaking of shoes, which is an abomination. (ibid.: 970)

With the wisdom of hindsight it is easy enough to sense the arbitrariness of nineteenth century notions of disorder, but here is a more contemporary managerial classification of order that equally allows the recognition of disorder and shows the relationship between the two. This example comes from a paper by John Patterson (1993), Director of the Department of Health and Community Services in the Australian State of Victoria. His Department funded a number of the Health Centres whose managers I have interviewed. Patterson calls, in terms that evoke both Douglas and Beeton, for a '*cleansing* of inter-governmental arrangements' (ibid.: 3) as part of microeconomic reform of Australia's health and welfare system. From what dirt are these 'arrangements' to be cleansed?

Patterson is quite clear about this: any constraint on the operation of market conditions:

> Standard theory says that if we take an optimized system and introduce one binding constraint we reduce the total utility generated by that system by some amount. We are then in the world of 'second best'. (ibid.: 21)

With a 'binding constraint', the optimized system of the market is no longer optimized. It (and 'we') are second best, not even worst, but somewhere in between, in a system now described by Patterson as 'corrupt' (ibid.: 21). A corrupted market results in:

- strong vested interests in keeping it corrupted;
- bizarre production/consumption behaviour; and
- unpredictable transitional conditions while it is being corrupted. (ibid.: 21)

The clarity of the system is made confused and ambiguous by 'vested interests' that are not governed by it. Behaviour becomes 'bizzare', conditions become 'unpredictable'. Worse perhaps, the market becomes 'transitional' – an in-between non-system. There is hope however. Patterson proposes that we 'uncorrupt the health and welfare market' by letting loose 'the chill winds of competition'. This will result in a cleansed environment where 'there is no individual negotiation, are no games, no deals, and no favourites' (ibid.: 30). In such an optimal environment, 'there is not much fun left in being a bureaucrat', because bureaucracy is constrained from playing off vested interests and manipulating unpredictable conditions.

From this extract we can easily set out Patterson's version of the abominations of Leviticus:

Table 6.1 *Patterson's version of the abominations of Leviticus*

Clean	Unclean
standard theory	binding constraint
maximum utility	unpredictable conditions, bizzare behaviour
uncorrupted markets	corrupted markets
unrestricted markets	vested interests, individual negotiation
chill winds	fun, games, deals and favourites
competition	bureaucracy
optimized system	transitional

The unclean is anything that muddies the clarity of standard theory and inhibits its smooth operation. It is matter out of place that makes it ambiguous whether market forces are operating or not. It is fun and games that would take the bite out of the chill winds of competition. It is concerns that are not clearly about utility, concerns that are individual, unpredictable, that could be about anything at all. Once this rubbish is put out however, Patterson claims, in an image at once evoking purity and victory, Victoria's hospital system 'will show a clean pair of heels to the rest of Australia's public hospitals this year and next' (ibid.: 30).

For Patterson, then, recognition of dirt and disorder is clearly relative to his sense of a clean and integral order. Making a system of order explicit, in turn makes dirt and disorder increasingly explicit for him. Ambiguity becomes, paradoxically, unambiguous, and so can be recognized and expelled.

We can see this happening even more clearly in the next example where the 'abomination' in question is actually a manager who is a bad house-keeper. One of the managers I interviewed was also on the management committee of the local school's before-and-after care centre. This committee, as it happened, was in the process of trying to sack the manager of the centre. The following extracts from the committee minutes show the attempt to delineate the manager, K, as disorderly, and K's attempts to resist this. The struggle takes place around a new advance booking system for using the centre, introduced by the committee to allow it to plan for the number of staff to be employed:

Vivian documented a number of concerns about how K had not supported or assisted in the implementation of the new system. These concerns are summarized:

- *problems with fee relief forms.* The Centre makes claims for government subsidies based on these fee relief applications . . . The folder containing the Centre's existing set of these forms appear to now be lost. Vivian recalls last seeing the folder when she returned it to K, and it was placed on top of a cupboard.
- *discrepancies in receipts.* K writes the receipts for fees. There are two copies of each receipt kept by the Centre. Yet there are differences in the amounts shown on the 2 copies in some cases (adjustments were made on the Bookkeeper's copy but not on the Treasurer's)
  The totals of receipts does [sic] not add up correctly
  There are differences in the amounts of cash received and the totals from the receipts
- *booking forms* The Centre has run out of booking forms on a few occasions. Vivian reported one occasions [sic] where K complained about this – rather than looked ahead and got forms copied . . .
  The attendance sheets for the week 10–17th were totally illegible, so that it is not possible to be sure that the right amounts have been charged for that week

The introduction of a formal system of booking lets the committee see instances where K has undermined order. K's actions – the lost folder of fee relief applications, the absence of application forms, the discrepancies in receipts, the difference between receipts and cash, running out of booking forms, complaining about running out of forms, illegible attendance sheets – all create ambiguity. They constantly blur the clarity of the booking system, making it unworkable. At the same time, the clarity of the system makes K's ambiguity and disorder clear, and the committee actually uses the system to do this. It defines their own sense of order, and so defines disorder. K's disorder is not an isolated event; it is a by-product of a systematic ordering which the booking system allows to be made explicit, and which orders the committee in relation to her.

Rubbish is Relative

If order and disorder are related, then what is recognized as disorder will vary with what is taken to be order. Neither will be given absolutely, and they may even change places. Interestingly, in the last example, the minutes give a glimpse that, from K's point of view, the booking system is 'rubbish' that should not intrude on her order:

> Sue reported an incident where K had responded to a query about the new booking system in a way which did not take any responsibility for it.

She does not see it as having anything to do with her as a manager. As Douglas (1966: 2) puts it: 'There is no such thing as absolute dirt: it exists in the eye of the beholder'.

Game (1994: 47) has written suggestively about this relativity of order and disorder, purity and impurity, in academic work:

> what is dirt with respect to a certain system of academic work is 'organization' itself, what is frequently dismissively referred to as 'administration'.

The academic administrator might imagine that she is creating order, but to academics she is simply the subordinate who cleans up their mess, and like the servants in Mrs Beeton's household, is a potential source of pollution, muddying the notion of what a university is really about:

> I might imagine myself as engaged in purification rituals, keeping pollution at bay, 'cleaning up practices in the department', 'keeping the paper moving', 'maintaining an empty desk', whilst academics regard my work as polluting to the pursuit of higher things, the purity of intellectual endeavours, neither generating nor moving paper. (ibid.: 48)

We can also see this relativity at work in the clean/unclean table derived from the Patterson paper. The grouping of elements like 'constraint', 'unpredictable', 'bureaucracy, 'fun' under 'unclean' has an inherent instability that could see any of these elements shift to the 'clean' side of the table. Patterson is, after all, himself a bureaucrat who clearly has fun constraining other bureaucrats. Moreover, the bureaucrats and 'vested interests' that created binding constraints on Patterson's market would not have seen themselves as proponents of disorder and corruption. One system's 'regulation' becomes another's 'constraint'. The very order that

Patterson is propounding disorders this manager of a large health service in South Australia:

> The thing that I dislike most is that I feel there's a movement, certainly in South Australia, to business management, and they're talking much more around contestability and contracting and the purchaser/provider stuff and about us needing to be ... not just money managers. I don't mind money management per se ... but, business management? ... It could drive me out. Yep. It hasn't impinged on my role yet. It's talked about more as an idea. I feel more like a dinosaur in that situation, and if that's what it is and I'm fighting it all the time, then I don't want to stay around as a manager.

One person's move against corruption – removal of constraint on market conditions – is experienced by another as corrupting – as confusing the job with mere 'business'. The new environment has a vaguely destabilizing effect, first experienced as 'a movement', and 'they're talking'. Something is changing, unsettling her management space, muddling it and making it unclear. Already she is feeling positioned as extinct, 'a dinosaur', a reject from today's order.

Mess as Management

Recognizing the relativity between order and disorder has led some contemporary writers on management to reverse the role of the effective manager: rather than custodian and creator of order, the postmodern manager is also supposed to be a source of disorder. Hamel and Prahalad (1989: 63) thus reverse the 1970s and 1980s corporate wisdom about the value of strategic planning, claiming that 'as 'strategy' has blossomed, the competitiveness of Western companies has withered'. If blossoming is really withering then order is really disorder, so Gergen (1992: 223) concludes that 'constant challenges to the smooth co-ordination of internal realities are essential to organizational vitality'. Disrupting order will restore life so that organization will blossom again.

It is a short step from valuing constant challenge to one's own order to asserting that the true role of the manager is to create disorder – the very reverse of Mrs Beeton's housekeeper. Peters (1987: 247) has most vigorously embraced this conclusion, quoting with approval the following anecdotes about Soichiro Honda, founder of the Honda Corporation:

> In the formative stages of his company Honda is variously reported to have tossed a geisha out a second-storey window, climbed inside a septic tank to retrieve a visiting supplier's false teeth (and subsequently placed the teeth in his mouth), appeared inebriated and in costume before a formal presentation to Honda's bankers requesting financing vital to the firm's survival (the loan was denied), hit a worker on the head with a wrench, and stripped naked before his engineers to assemble a motorcycle engine.

Drunk, violent, naked and steeped in sewage: in every way Honda physically reverses the traditional image of management. Equally he is the very embodiment of the new management whose task Peters describes thus:

> radically changing the organization's structure annually or even more frequently – it's a must. Changing all the procedures and then changing them again – another must. Smashing the market into bits, and then smashing it into even finer bits – a must as well. (ibid.: 468)

Peters' strategy, however, is not metaphoric, but a simple reversal. Order and disorder change places with the manager staying on the side that keeps him or her special and apart:

> the president is the main *dis*-organizer. Everybody 'manages' quite well: whenever anything goes wrong, they take immediate action to make sure nothing'll go wrong again. The problem is, nothing new will ever happen either. (Peters, 1992: 8–9)

Rubbish is Ambiguous

Peters' advice, however, does depend on an aspect of disorder that is potentially more relational. There is a power in what has been rejected as a threat to order, and this is an ambiguous power: it is not just threatening. Wynne (1987: 1) captures this feeling of ambiguity in wastes when he describes them as existing 'in a twilight zone where no clear "rational" definition of them can be given, within wide margins of uncertainty and variation'. 'Twilight' ambiguity suggests a possible movement towards either light or darkness. Douglas (1966: 94) describes this ambiguity as a potential for danger, but also for something more positive:

> disorder by implication is unlimited, no pattern has been realized in it, but its potential for patterning is infinite . . . it has potentiality. It symbolizes both danger and power.

Disorder, this suggests, is both destructive of order, and the material out of which order is created. Accordingly it may be experienced in either of two ways:

> First they [the 'bits and pieces' of rubbish] are recognizably out of place, a threat to good order, and so are regarded as objectionable and vigorously brushed away. At this stage they have some identity . . . they are dangerous. (ibid.: 160)

This is the stage where identifying wastes identifies ourselves as separate from them. Brushing them away confirms our identity. We have put out the rubbish. But there is a second stage when rubbish loses its identity:

So long as identity is absent, rubbish is not dangerous . . . In its last phase then, dirt shows itself as an apt symbol for creative formlessness. (ibid.: 161)

When I thought about the office that I occupied as manager, I found that I could have both these experiences of disorder from the same physical space. Here is what I wrote at the time:

If I glance over the surface of my desk I can see a sort of order. There is a cleared space to work on defined by a blotter, which isn't actually a blotter because nobody blots any more. It is a sort of executive throw-back that serves to mark out a clear working space. It is not exactly clear, however, because it becomes progressively covered with doodles made while thinking, or during boring phone calls. It also has phone numbers and other messages that I might jot down before transferring them to a message pad. At a certain point there gets to be so much accumulated doodling that I cannot find a number I just took down. Then I tear off the top page – it comes in the form of a large pad – and put it in the wastebasket. Sometimes I start a new pad merely because the old one looks disgusting. The corner of the whole pad has gotten dog-eared, which annoys me, so it is pinned down with a paper clip – a temporary, patched-up order that suffices for the moment.

In front of the pad are three trays. These are supposed to organize the documents I am immediately working with, and they do, although not altogether in the way they were meant to. The central one is the 'active' tray, with the documents I am currently working on. In fact, only the top papers are active. The rest has settled like sediment, to be chucked out or filed once in a while. Other 'active' documents also drift around the environs of the blotter.

The left hand tray, because it is near the entrance of my office, is the 'in' tray. But, again, much of what goes in never makes it to the active tray, so only the top layer, about an inch or so, works as the real 'in' tray. The rest is also sediment. The right hand tray contains articles to read, but it is really for articles I never get around to reading, and sometimes I place 'active' files on top of the articles when there's nowhere else to put them.

What this desk surface amounts to, then, is a sort of active or live top layer, resting on a sedimentary layer of material that may get activated, but is progressively becoming irrelevant. Much of it may end up in the wastepaper basket. Some of it may eventually get filed, away from my office, so I am not physically overwhelmed by all this material.

As I look around the office this arrangement of active, shading into sedimentary space, is replicated everywhere. For instance, on the partition in front of me is a contact list for my committee. I refer to this all the time. Around it are sticky yellow labels with phone numbers that I use. Beyond this area, that I can comfortably read from my desk, is a penumbra of fading notices, postcards and forgotten newspaper clippings, all of this pinned or stuck over a laminated poster whose once striking postbox red is mutating to a sort of washed-out brown where it is exposed to the direct sunlight that sweeps this wall too early for me to see it, except at the very height of summer.

Reading over this description even now, two years later, I am appalled at the shabbiness and disorder it conveys. A good manager would have swept all this away and started again. But there is another reaction also.

Recalling how my office felt to me through this description, there is a sort of comfortable softness about it. It is not exactly like a rubbish heap, because it is not *exactly* rubbish I was surrounded by. It is an accumulated near-past that in some moods could seem more like the litter of nesting material. Up to a certain point it *feels* comfortable, regardless of how it *looks*. It is like a sort of outer skin or a shell containing me. Not exactly me, but my shape.

This reminds me of what Bachelard (1969: 102–3) has written so potently about nests and their significance: of how the nest is shaped and compacted into a felt-like padding by nothing else than the pressure of the bird's body to produce 'a centre of animal life concealed by the vast volume of vegetable life'. The nest, says Bachelard, stirs up our sense of a secure home 'modelled by fine touches', which make a surface originally bristling and composite into one that is smooth and soft. The human being, he claims, 'likes to "withdraw into his corner", and . . . it gives him physical pleasure to do so' (ibid.: 91).

That structure of an active layer, floating on a sediment that can still be reactivated, but is gradually becoming rubbish, seems to be determined by the reach of my senses: what I can immediately touch, or what I can see without moving too greatly. It is a span of comfortable control, as if my body does not end at my skin, but about an inch below that layer that is within visible or tactile range. And the material under that is shaped by that body, like padding around it.

Rubbish here has lost its identity and so allows the creation of an order of bodily comfort that can modify or even override the visible order of a 'well-managed' office. Through a level of disorder I create myself as 'at home' in the office, though the level is such that, in certain moods, it can threaten to invade my sense of being a manager. Here we see Douglas' two stages in the recognition of rubbish, although not necessarily in chronological order. At times I recognize this situation as disorderly, intruding on the clean space of my ideal office, sapping at my integrity as an ideal manager. At other times the bits and pieces lose that identity, and so become material to form into a different office, one in which I can feel at home in my body.

Order and Emptiness

The ambiguity of disorder – its potential for creativity – does not mean that all rubbish is immediately valuable, as if the items in Patterson's list had simply changed places. The issue, we find once again, is a metaphoric relationship that works as experience. Without a relationship between ourselves, order and disorder, and the possibility of traffic between, no living order would be possible. A living order creates its own imperative: rubbish has to be put out. But such an order is also permeable, or it would not live beyond its own rejection of rubbish. The 'pure beginning' that

Bachelard holds necessary for creativity would become a pure end. It would be fixed and dead. Douglas (1966: 162) recognizes this when she declares that 'purity is the enemy of change, of ambiguity and compromise':

> The quest for purity is pursued by rejection. It follows that when purity is not a symbol but something lived, it must be poor and barren. (ibid.: 161)

Wallace Stevens gives us a striking observation of this. Taking a last look at his bachelor's room on the day of his wedding, he remarks:

> Yesterday's disorder has turned into the strict arrangements of emptiness. (quoted in Richardson, 1986: 365)

Disorder has been ordered, but the order only makes him feel empty. There is only a room now, not a home, still less a nest. He no longer inhabits it, and it no longer inhabits him. Its order contains nothing that he can live in. Pure order like this is the product of 'putting out the rubbish' until there is nothing left: it is not an invitation but a closure. Too often management represents itself as living such a closure. The following manager, from whom I have already quoted on planning, has no sense of ambiguity about his office:

– What's your office like? Is it tidy?
  Sometimes it's completely clean sometimes covered in rubbish.
– How do you like it?
  Clean. Nothing there.
– Why?
  Paper means you have to do something. It makes demands. You have to respond.
– So you feel your freedom is controlled by paper?
  Definitely. It really shits me.
– What else shits you?
  Staff. They always want something.
– So they control you, like paper?
  Yes. They make demands. They want this and that. But they're like children. You never really satisfy them.
– You could never manage to satisfy everyone's needs?
  Never.

What constitutes dirt for this manager, what 'shits' him, is any outside demand at all, be it administration or other staff. A space free of demand – a completely free and empty office – would be a space of freedom for him, but what the content of this freedom would be is not at all clear. It is purity only defined by rejection, a freedom in relation to nothing.

Mrs Beeton offers another instance of the emptiness of pure order. If we recall her injunction to the Mistress to begin her day with a ritual of cleaning, we may feel that those 'cold or tepid baths' are as much a punishment as a renewal of the body. Pursuing this interpretation, her 'spirit' may be what rules the house because her body has been repressed or subtracted. This same repression is evident in her prescriptions for social life. Even in dealing with friends, behaviour is to be 'cleaned up' so that the smooth social surface is as untarnished as the well polished plate on the dinner table:

> In conversation, trifling occurrences, such as small disappointments, petty annoyances, and other every-day incidents should never be mentioned to your friends. (1861: 4)

The suppression of apparent trivia – the rejection of 'bits and pieces' – means that the mistress is never committed to a conversation beyond her conscious control, even when visiting her friends:

> During these visits, the manners should be easy and cheerful, and the subjects of conversation such as may be readily terminated. (ibid.: 10)

Danger lurks in the form of emotion or over-involvement that might threaten smoothness:

> Serious discussions or arguments are to be altogether avoided, and there is much danger and impropriety in expressing opinions of those persons and characters with whom, perhaps, there is but a slight acquaintance. (ibid.: 10)

Through an over-zealous cleaning up and control of friendship, the pleasant and sociable borders on the vacuous.[5]

That 'cleaning up' of everything that might move, motivate, and engage, is so prevalent in management that it usually passes unnoticed. Returning to the minutes of the after-care meeting I discussed earlier I learned that the meeting itself was in fact highly emotional, tense, and argumentative. None of this emotion is evident in the 'true record' of the meeting, which reads like a series of logical steps leading to an inevitable conclusion. I was informed that great care was actually taken to create this impression when the minutes were composed. Any sense of emotion was quite consciously excluded so the decision would appear to be a rational rather than an emotional one. Ironically it was this very level of emotion, the cumulative sense of disgust and frustration, that led to the movement to sack the manager in the first place. Emotion is disorderly to management, and so no evidence of emotion must adhere to its actions. Its very absence affirms that management has taken place. Emotion has been put out along with the rubbish.

'We Need That Waste'

What does management do with the rubbish that it puts out? In an ideally managed world that is not an issue: waste does not exist. We can see this fantasy at work on the cover of the Sydney Water Board's *Wastewater Information Kit* (Wastewater Source Control Branch 1994), as shown in Figure 6.1, supplied to my organization when we wished to clarify our responsibilities for waste disposal. As an instance of the disembodiment of management, this cover makes an interesting pair with the *Toolkit* cover from Chapter 1.

Within the circle of the words 'Wastewater Source Control Branch' sits a committee of suited men and women seemingly engaged in civilized bureaucratic discussion. They are seated at a table, or, rather, table top, because nothing of the people or table is depicted below. The committee is actually cut off at the 'waist', altogether removing those parts of their bodies that produce 'waste'. Separated from this semi-disembodied committee by an expanse of paper whose aggressively textured surface signals its recycled status, are two blue borders depicting stylized waves and fish: a cleaned up nature as the healthy outcome of good management. Waste is not depicted at all, except in the grain of the recycled paper, the mark of successful waste management because it is no longer waste. All waste has been managed away; there is nothing over after management. But where, I wonder, do the bottom halves of those managers go? Where is their space? Once again we meet, this time in the guise of a manageable environment, an order that has already half-forgotten its own body.[6]

Cixous (in Cixous and Clément, 1986) offers a quite different account of waste. Waste is possibility where we can live in excess of our own or other people's order. In particular, it allows women to live beyond the phallocentric order imposed on them. She speaks of 'writing the body', a writing that allows the unmanageable to enter language through a body that speaks beyond a self-recognized identity. It lets something escape from a controlling phallocentric discourse. Speaking of the fear and discomfort most women experience when addressing a gathering, she sees this very discomfort as an index of something that can go beyond the presentation of a poised and polished self:

> She exposes herself. Really she makes what she thinks materialize carnally, she conveys meaning with her body. She inscribes what she is saying because she does not deny unconscious drives the unmanageable part they play in speech. (ibid.: 92)

Language, embodied in this way, Cixous claims, exceeds the managed, cleaned up order of public discourse, the 'thin thread, dry and taut,' of the orator:

> We like uneasiness, questioning. There is waste in what we say. We need that waste. To write is always to make allowances for superabundance and uselessness while slashing the exchange value that keeps the spoken word on its track. (ibid.: 95)

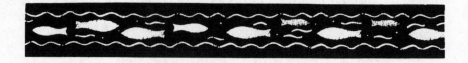

Information Kit

Figure 6.1 *Cover Illustration: Wastewater Source Control Branch (1994)*
Information Kit

In the body of Cixous' speaker there is something that exceeds the
controlled order of the speaker. That excess is the glimpse of possibility
beyond a self-identity that has become empty. Her body is already
experiencing a different possibility of organization even as it expels the

order of the accomplished speaker, just as my body in my office experienced a different sort of organization in what was disorder to the eye of management. 'Waste' here is rubbish from the perspective of assured self-identity, but 'superabundance' from the perspective of a glimpsed different order. It is the ambiguous and necessary excess in which a living order can be created or recognized as possible. If a writer has only a blank sheet of paper, out of what will she or he write?

Disorder as Metaphoric

Disorder demands to be managed. It is disturbing, offensive, disgusting. The order of our body rejects it, and in rejecting, we affirm that order. Without a sense of disorder we would have no feeling for our boundaries, no experience of wholeness or integrity, no sense of body at all. Disorder is a by-product of our sense of order, but order is also a by-product of our sense of disorder. We cannot have one without the other. Effective managing, therefore, will always be involved in handling disorder and rubbish. Managers can deny or object to this function, but there is no absolute order to which they can retreat. A John Patterson may, for example, have secretaries and cleaners to handle the rubbish and detritus around him, but his own management task, as we saw, revolves around a project of cleaning up and expelling disorder. He may not see his project as housekeeping, but that, essentially, is what it is. Housekeeping is always part of managing.

But housekeeping may be experienced in different ways. It may be an unceasing battle to expel disorder, a battle that must be renewed each day as the detritus of that day accumulates once again. Such a housekeeping, however, exclusively pursued, is merely the other side of that desire for a self that is pure and unconnected with disorder. It is a housekeeping of a self that would not acknowledge its own housekeeping. It is a wearying and demeaning task because it creates a self that is merely absence, and that would, besides, deny the activity that creates it. It is a non-metaphoric housekeeping – an 'X' based on separation from 'not-X', whose only identity is that separation, while denying the very labour that brings the separation about. Douglas (1966: 162) nicely puts the paradox involved here:

> The final paradox of the search for purity is that it is an attempt to force experience into logical categories of non-contradiction. But experience is not amenable and those who make the attempt find themselves led into contradictions.

There is, however, another way of experiencing housekeeping. It can be an affirming gesture, as in Calvino's putting out the rubbish. In affirming a sense of wholeness and integrity it creates a new day as possible: it puts us in relation to possibility. The order that this housekeeping creates is not then empty, but an order in relation to what is beyond it. But that beyond may be its own rubbish, now recognized as the formless stuff of creation. What is recognized metaphorically as not-X always has the possibility of becoming X.

Recognizing this possibility, it must be reiterated, does not imply a simple reversal, where X and not-X change places. Once again, Simmel's door is helpful in understanding this relation. When the infinite formlessness of the outside threatens to invade the hut, dissolving its integrity, we may, recognizing the threat, vigorously clear it out, reaffirming our boundaries and shutting the door. That is one relation to disorder that Douglas describes. The other is that, no longer threatened, and secure in our sense of ourselves, we open the door and stride out into the possibility of what we may become. But it is neither the inside nor the outside that is us, but the articulation: we embody both. Recognizing this, we can manage disorder – metaphorically.

Notes

1 Sheldrake (1989: 321), in discussing the evolutionary creativity of morphic fields, finds such a 'pure beginning' in the emergence of new fields:

No amount of creativity expressed within the context of any morphic field at any level of complexity can explain the appearance of that field itself for the very first time.

Nature itself, to exercise freedom, must also, it seems, perform that 'difficult transcendence of knowledge'.

2 This vacancy that is not empty also recalls Figure 2.8 of the *Ten Cow-Herding Pictures*.

3 For writer Carmel Bird (1994: 45), being a writer in front of a clean sheet of paper is just this separation from the maternal and the domestic:

Real writers don't have mothers. Real writers know they might succeed with their writing and they might fail, and they are prepared to take responsibility for the success or failure of the work. So they get to work. They face up to the icy challenge of the paper and they write.

For Julius Caesar, an indicator that the Gauls were barbarians was their failure to leave domesticity behind when they went to work. Here he describes the Gallic army on the move:

There were besides about six thousand men of various sorts, as well as domestics and children: but there was no organization, no defined authority, as everyone followed his own judgement and they all travelled on confidently, in the same informal way as they had always done. (1967: 61)

4 There is something of tragic irony in Isabella's death from puerperal fever at the age of 28. As Spain (1948: 245) comments:

Puerperal fever in the [18]60s was not considered due to anything but bad luck. It is only recently, through the work of Semmelweiss, that it has been established that the initial causes are dirt and neglect.

She may well have been killed by the dirt and disorder that her whole enterprise of management was designed to keep at bay.

5 James Ivory's film *Remains of the Day* (1993) offers a moving account of a butler (played by Sir Anthony Hopkins) who could have come straight from the pages of Mrs Beeton. His life is so self-effacing that he is left with no remainder from which he could begin a more passionate relationship.

6 A less 'clean cut' version of waste is starting to appear in literature on waste management. Wynne (1987), for example, has criticized the implicitly waste-free universe, not because it represents an ideal that can never be precisely obtained, but because it misunderstands the way waste is produced. Hazard and waste, he goes on to say, are:

not just imprecise or 'statistically fuzzy' – they are *fundamentally* ambiguous. Their intrinsic physical meaning is not given and objectively predetermined in nature; it is always incomplete, and has to be completed by social construction. (ibid.: 8)

MANAGING AND ART

Cixous' claim that 'we need that waste' and Douglas' warning about the emptiness of purity alert us to the fact that if order and cleanliness work metaphorically, they re-embody us in relation to what is beyond them – to what is disorderly and unclean. A disembodying management fails to create order relationally, resulting in, on the one hand, an empty order, and, on the other, a denial of its own process of ordering, resulting in a housekeeping that is unproductive and demanding. A.S. Byatt's (1993) story, *Art Work*, explores both the vacancy of an empty order and the unproductiveness of the activity that brings it about; but more than that, it relates order and disorder in a metaphoric movement that goes beyond them to create something new.

Art Work begins with an account of a black and white reproduction, in a book on Matisse by Sir Lawrence Gower, of 'Le Silence habité des maisons'. The picture depicts two figures, perhaps a mother and child, seated at a table in front of 'six huge panes of window'. Matisse effects, according to Gower 'the reconciliation which is only within the reach of great painters in old age'. (31–2) The theme of relating and reconciling art and the work of housekeeping pervades Byatt's story.

Art Work is set at 49 Alma Rd, home and workplace of Debbie and Robin Dennison and their children, Jamie and Natasha. 'Le silence' is not much evident in this 'maison'. Omnipresent in the household through the sound of her Hoover is Mrs Brown, the cleaner.

Debbie, the design editor of *A Woman's Place*, is working at home. Her son, Jamie, has chicken pox, and the doctor may or may not come at any moment. Upstairs, in an attic converted to a studio, is her husband Robin, an artist, although not a commercially successful one. Debbie would like to be an artist too, but of necessity she has become the breadwinner.

Mrs Brown, preceded by the whine of the Hoover, is the centre of Debbie's juggling act to manage the household. Without her, 'Debbie's world would not hold together' (39). Mrs Brown deals with the rubbish and disorder of Debbie's life:

Mrs Brown washes Debbie's underwear and tidies Debbie's desk, putting Debbie's letters, private and official, threatening and secret, in tidy heaps. Mrs

Brown counts the bottles and sweeps up the broken glass after parties, though she does not partake of the festive food. Mrs Brown changes Debbie's sheets. (41–2)

To know someone's rubbish – what they must put out in order to reaffirm themselves – creates a particular intimacy:

If Mrs Brown is not Debbie's friend, she is the closest person to Debbie on earth, excluding perhaps the immediate family. (41)

While Mrs Brown is introduced through the pervasive sound of her cleaning, her visual appearance, and particularly her apparel, is anything but tidy:

Mrs Brown's clothes were, and are, flowery and surprising, jumble sale remnants, rejects and ends of lines, rainbow-coloured jumpers made from the ping-pong-ball-sized unwanted residues from other people's knitting. She came for her interview in a not too clean (but not too dirty) film star's trench-coat . . . [she] divested herself of the trench-coat, revealing pantaloons made of some kind of thick cream-coloured upholstery linen, wonderfully traversed by crimson open-mouthed Indian flowers and birds of paradise and tendrils of unearthly creepers, and a royal-blue jumper embroidered all over with woollen daisies, white marguerites, orange black-eyed Susans. (40)

Mrs Brown's disorder, however, is a fertile disorder – a creativity akin to nature that is emphasized by her preference for going barefoot in the house.

At the moment the doctor arrives, Debbie has to intervene in a dispute between her husband, Robin, and Mrs Brown. Robin is in a rage because Mrs Brown, in cleaning up his studio, has used a bowl, which 'as anyone can see, is a work of art' (46), for a rubbish receptacle:

'Look', cries Robin. The bowl, both sumptuously decorated and dusty, contains a few random elastic bands, a chain of paperclips, an obscure plastic cog from some tiny clock, a battered but unused stamp, two oil pastels, blue and orange, a piece of dried bread, a very short length of electric wire, a dead chrysanthemum, three coloured thumbtacks (red, blue, green), a single lapis cufflink, an electric bulb with a burnt patch on its curve, two india rubbers, a dead bluebottle and two live ants, running in circles, possibly busy, possibly frantically lost.

'Her habits are filthy', says Robin. (46–7)

Mrs Brown, for Robin, *is* dirt and disorder, although his own studio 'which is not the habitation of a tidy man' is disorderly enough to Debbie's eyes, and even the disputed bowl is described as 'both sumptuously decorated and dusty'. Robin, however, knows where the distinctions are to be made:

Dirt is dirt, and personal things, things in use, are things in use. All it requires is intelligence. (47)

Robin 'has ritualized his life dangerously', following in this his father who had particular regard to the distinction 'between his own untouchable "things" and other people's, especially the cleaning-lady's "filth"' (57). Robin's desire for separation from impurity is represented both in the physical structure of the house, which literally supports his studio attic, and in the familial structure, whereby Debbie supports and manages him, herself supported by Mrs Brown. That structure, through which Robin has ordered himself as an artist separated from the world's distraction and impurity, is not without its effect on his art. His paintings, which emphasize the purity of colour and unique distinctness of individual objects separated from their surroundings, are bordering dangerously on the trivial and repetitive:

> He painted small bright things in large expanses of grey and buff and beige. Everyone said, 'He's *got* something,' or more dubiously, 'He's got *something*.' Probably not enough, they qualified this, silently to themselves, but Robin heard them well enough, for all that. (56)

If Robin's separation from disorder has left an emptiness that diminishes his creativity, Debbie's frantic and anxious management leaves no clear space for her own. Between looking after her children, doing her job, managing her husband, and keeping Mrs Brown on side, her own interest in wood engraving is now only a ghost that quietly haunts her:

> Her fingers remembered the slow, careful work in the wood, with a quiet grief that didn't diminish, but was manageable. She hated Robin because he never once mentioned the unmade wood engravings . . . Debbie continued to love Robin, whilst hating him because of the woodcuts, because of the extent of his absence of interest in how she managed the house, the children, the money, her profession, his needs and wants, and because of his resolute attempts to unsettle, humiliate, or drive away Mrs Brown, without whom all Debbie's balancing acts would clatter and fall in wounding disarray. (54–5)

Her time is filled, but she is left empty and resentful. Her own ordering does not order her. It separates her from a remembered body that still lingers in her fingers and that hates what would destroy it. It prevents any development of the sort of metaphoric movement that is glimpsed in a striking passage where she daubs calamine on her son Jamie's chicken-pox:

> He has the same skin [as his mother and sister] too, but at the moment it is a wonderfully humped and raised terrain of rosy peaks and hummocks, mostly the pink of those boring little begonias with fleshy leaves, but some raging into salmon-deeps and some extinct volcanoes, with umber and ochre crusts . . . Debbie stood him on a coffee table and swabbed and painted him with calamine lotion, creating a kind of streaked sugar or plaster of Paris manikin . . . Debbie would have like to paint him all over, with fern-green cake dye and cochineal,

if that would have distracted or assuaged him, but she had to get the piece she was writing done. (36–7)

The texture of Jamie's skin, which could read like an outbreak of uncleanliness from Leviticus, stimulates Debbie aesthetically, so that a mundane moment of household management suggests an occasion of playful creativity – an occasion she puts off because of the further demands of life-management.

It is that ability to recognize disorder as, in Douglas' (1966: 161) phrase, 'an apt symbol for creative formlessness' that distinguishes Mrs Brown, the cleaner, as the one who manages most successfully. One form of Mrs Brown's polluting presence, for Robin, is making things for the family: tea-cosies, cushion covers and jumpers for the children. These, like her own flamboyant clothes, are to him 'the epitome of tat'. He attempts to make her understand about colour, but to little effect. She has her own theory, as she expounds to Debbie:

'They always told us, didn't they, the teachers and grans, orange and pink, they make you blink, blue and green should not be seen, mauve and red cannot be wed, but I say, they're all there, the colours. God made 'em all, and mixes 'em all in His creatures, what exists goes together somehow or other, don't you think Mrs Dennison?'

'Well, yes, but there are rules too, you know, Mrs Brown, how to get certain effects, there are *rules*, complementary colours and things . . .'

'I'm learning all that. He tells me, when I move his things by accident, or whatever. Fascinating.' (Byatt 1993: 61)

Mrs Brown experiences colour, rather than combining it through rules. Ironically, it is her theory that wins out – as art. When Debbie covers a story for her magazine at a gallery that has rejected Robin's work, she arrives to find the whole space 'transformed into a kind of soft, even squashy, brilliantly coloured Aladdin's Cave' (77):

The cavern has a crazy kind of resemblance to a lived-in room. Chests of drawers, made of orange boxes covered with patchworks of wallpaper, from vulgar silver roses to William Morris birds, from Regency plum stripes to Laura Ashley pink sprigs, reveal half-open treasure chests with mazy compartments containing crazy collections of things. White bone buttons. Glass stoppers. Chicken bones. Cufflinks, all single. Medicine bottles with lacquered labels, full of iridescent beads and codliver-oil capsules. Pearlised plastic poppet beads and sunflower seeds, doll's teaspoons and drifts of variegated tea leaves and dead rose-petals. Sugar mice, some half-chewed. String, bright green, waxed red, hairy brown, running from compartment to compartment. (78)

The artist, of course, is Mrs Brown, now known to Debbie for the first time by her full name: Sheba Brown. Her work as a cleaner provides the materials for her art, as a promotional brochure at the exhibition explains:

She gets her materials from everywhere – skips, jumble sales, cast-offs, going through other people's rubbish, cleaning up after school fêtes. (85)

Sheba Brown's intimate contact with rubbish gives her work a vitality that Robin's more exclusive ordering lacks and that Debbie's frantic juggling leaves no time for. Her work, in fact, celebrates the opulence and fertility of domestic space through playing with what it has rejected. Her cleaning is not an end in itself, but something that relates her to possibility.

As it happens, exposure to Sheba Brown's exhibition creates a slight twist in the lives of Debbie and Robin, enough to spur Debbie to go back to woodcuts, and Robin to develop a different style of painting with 'a new kind of loosed, slightly savage energy' (90) and 'a recurring motif of a dark, glaring face with red eyes and a protruding red tongue: that looks suspiciously like Mrs Brown'. Disorder has entered his art, stimulating a new kind of life.

8

MANAGING BEYOND MANAGEMENT

Let us re-visit that quotation from Lefebvre (1991: 405) with which we began the first chapter:

> The whole of (social) space proceeds from the body, even though it so metamorphoses the body that it may forget it altogether – even though it may separate itself so radically from the body as to kill it. The genesis of a far-away order can be accounted for only on the basis of the order that is nearest to us – namely, the order of the body.

If we want to understand what we do when we manage, Lefebvre tells us that we must begin by asking what we have done with our own bodies. But the matter cannot end there. The last three chapters have shown how the process of organizing involves the embodiment of the manager as ordered, and how this process is metaphoric, because metaphor organizes a lived relationship between ourselves and an 'outside', allowing each to permeate the other. But if managing has a movement of organizing the self through an ordering of space outside, it also encompasses a contrary movement, organizing an 'outside' on the basis of that self. Something, as Lefebvre puts it, 'proceeds from the body': a 'space' that is also an 'order'. Something exceeds the body's order and goes beyond it.

It should be clear, however, when talking about movement beyond the body, that I am talking about an emphasis only. Whether there is an embodying of order, or a creation of order from the body, there is always a relation. I can create order through embodiment because, in Merleau-Ponty's succinct formulation, 'things have an internal equivalent in me: they arouse in me a carnal formula of their presence' (1964: 164). And the reverse is also true: I have an external equivalent in things: I arouse in them a carnal formula of my presence. But this relation between my body and the order it creates means that the results of my managing also re-create me. Having an effect on the outside world is a more 'obvious' movement of managing, and indeed, any current textbook on management would claim that this is all that managing is about: change, results, achieving objectives. What is usually neglected is the embodied basis on which this ordering of the outside is made, a basis of which Lefebvre reminds us.

Suppressing that bodily connection makes the focus on results and objectives in management deceptively obvious. But embodied managing does not end in a result – in producing an order – because that result flows back to re-embody us within it. In a real sense, then, successful managing never ends – not in the workaholic sense of unending competition – but because it is a continuing relation between the body and its order. Movement towards an 'outside' turns back to encompass an 'inside'. We can notice this movement of return even as the following managers characterize management as their influence on the outside:

> everything I do is always around having something finished . . . about having a result at the end of it. And I think that that's what drives me in management. There's a big challenge there in actually changing things and to see that come to fruition and happen is what I get out of it.

> I like influencing change in a positive way. Where there are areas in managing that allow me to do that, I enjoy them greatly.

> You're performing well when you've participated in or led, usually led, a change to something that's produced a positive result. That's from your own subjective perception of positive result. That's the way you measure, I measure, success.

Each of these accounts speaks of making a change to something other, to 'a far-away order' in Lefebvre's phrase, of 'having something finished', of 'influencing change', of producing 'a positive result'. Nevertheless, each of them also implicates themselves in that change: 'what I get out of it'; 'I enjoy them greatly'; 'your own subjective perception of a positive result'. The outside here is not something entirely separate. While it is the movement towards that outside that they emphasize, that movement returns to, and encompasses them as well. These results are not just accumulations in an 'out there' that is no part of them.

This movement of return that encompasses the mover allows us to put a rather different interpretation on the concept of 'result.' We saw in Chapter 5 how the management by objectives movement envisaged the purpose of management as reaching certain pre-determined end points or outcomes. We also saw that the process of planning this way was only meaningful if it created the planners themselves as organized. That planning process must create an order of the body that can form the basis of a 'far-away' order. In the same way we can argue that the achievement of a 'far-away' order, or an objective, is only meaningful if it metaphorically includes us in that order. Results, as an imagined point in time, work only if they are the metaphoric index of a new ordering; they fail if they are an end in and for themselves.

Embodying Order

Results are only organizing if they are organizing in relation to us, if they flow back to embody us differently. Two experiences from the managing of a passion of mine, bushwalking, illustrate this. In the mid 1970s I went, with a group of friends, on a rafting trip down the Gordon River in south-west Tasmania. Not many people had done the trip at that time, so it aroused all the fear and excitement of going into the unknown. Possibly the most lasting memory of that journey – I can still feel it as I write, twenty years later – was lying back in the camping ground at Strahan, at the end of the trip, with the wind howling in the trees above my head, feeling a tremendous sense of completeness, as I recalled the journey in its entirety, from its first conception, through its realization, to the moment, then, when it was finally over. I was part of that river and that wilderness, and the wind howling overhead, and yet I had never felt so much myself. There was a sort of aesthetic perfection here, like a work of art. I was complete, and something was complete about the world.

The trip was triggered by a news item about the river on television, an item that ended with the comment that very few people had ventured into the country beyond the river's mouth. I had an immediate sense that I would like to go down that river. There was a metaphoric movement of affinity that connected me with it; it was a possibility I wanted to become. But it was only a lot of planning, many lists, and a minute examination of maps that gave me the confidence that the trip was a real possibility. It was that ordering, inspired by the original movement of affinity, that I then brought into the actual space of the river. I could move through the wilderness in a meaningful way because it responded to my own organization. It was strange and dangerous, but not altogether unreadable. It was not totally outside me. But because that reading was successful, I in turn felt part of something larger than myself. I was also re-embodied from that 'outside'. Metaphorically, I moved beyond myself through a dynamic relation between inside and outside.

The second experience also involved the fulfilment of a plan. I have an old, sepia-covered edition of *100 Walks in New South Wales* (Thomas, 1977), a book that has given me many ideas for interesting places to go. It worked for me as a list, helping to embody me as a walker. One day, however, I discovered that I had 'done' about a third of the walks. Having a strong obsessive streak I got some satisfaction ticking them off, and decided then and there to go on and do all 100. About seven years later I ticked off the 99th, and then the 100th walk. It was a disappointing experience, so much so that I did not even bother to make the last tick. It was disappointing because, by that time, a second edition of the book had come out, with many different walks. I had only done 100 walks in the first edition! This was very much someone else's list. And then, the 100th walk was nothing special, and in a way no different to the 99th or the 101st. I was only doing it because it was number 100. The actual walks had become items on the list, rather than the reverse. Ultimately there seemed something pointless and arbitrary in counting walks in this way – a quantity without quality. The accumulation produced no new whole; nothing exceeded the original ordering.

In contrast to the first experience, this one did not work metaphorically. While there was clearly an effect from following this list, in the sense that 100 walks happened, in a meaningful sense nothing much happened at all. The order I transferred was not an embodied order, and so failed to create new meaning. I did not make that 'outside' out of myself, and so, in turn, it did not become a part of me. I had related an order outside my body to a space outside my body: an outside to an outside.

A movement away from the body towards an outside is only successful if that outside is let 'in'. Simply imposing an order does not create organization. There is no flow between the body and its ordering. When there is flow, however, both terms are affected. My organization opened up the river to me, but in turn I too was opened up to be something beyond what I originally was. The achievement of a 'far-away' order, or an objective, is only meaningful if the metaphoric *relation* is still maintained. Where it is not, as in our second walking example, no meaningful order results.[1] Results, as an imagined point in time, work only if they are the metaphoric index of a new ordering; they fail if they are an end in and for themselves.

From Cleanliness to Godliness

Mrs Beeton, in that part of her book that goes beyond cleanliness and order, illustrates this relational movement between self and results. It is significant that, even when she is recognized as a legitimate writer on management, it is that very part of her work that is overlooked. Wensley (1996: 37) sums up her approach to management in three principles:

- setting an example and giving clear guidance to the staff;
- controlling the finances;
- applying the benefits of order and method in all management activities.

These principles cover the Mrs Beeton we discussed in Chapter 6, but this is, I would suggest, only, or less than, half the story. Mrs Beeton's management is by no means limited to creating the household as a clean and ordered body, but goes on to open a space beyond its own order, a space in which that body is then taken up and transported beyond itself. The ideal of order – the hope 'that everything may move smoothly' (Beeton, 1861: 23) – might be appropriate to that 'beautiful piece of mechanism' to which Mrs Beeton compares the human body 'materially considered' (ibid.: 1026), but a living body, she implies, is more than a mechanism. Cleanliness and order are only next to godliness, not the godly state itself. It is food and eating that take household management beyond preparation of a smooth surface, beyond the world 'materially considered'. But it is precisely at this point that Wensley (1996: 45) cuts off the story when he concludes:

Nearly 140 years later, it is perhaps her comments on the nature of good practical management . . . that stand the test of time: more so than some of her guidance on cooking or etiquette

The vast bulk of *The Book of Household Management* is actually about food: 1,500 or so recipes, plus menus, table layouts and information on different types of food, including even chemical changes during cooking. What makes food so important? If cleaning separates the household from natural squalor, it is dining that confers civilization:

The nation which knows how to dine has learnt the leading lesson of progress. It implies both the will and the skill to reduce to order, and surround with idealisms and graces, the more material conditions of human existence; and whenever that will and that skill exist, life cannot be wholly ignoble. (ibid.: 905)

Two stages of managing are identified here: first reduction to order of material conditions, and then, surrounding them by idealisms and graces. It is only with the latter stage that life becomes 'not wholly ignoble' because it is here that, as Mrs Beeton puts it, materiality 'assumes new forms', and it does this, first and foremost, through cookery. Cooking becomes a creative play with food that transforms it as if by magic, and the magician of the Victorian household is the cook:

Everything that is edible, and passes under the hands of the cook, is more or less changed, and assumes new forms. Hence the influence of that functionary is immense upon the happiness of a household. (ibid.: 39)

Cooking becomes a metaphoric process that transforms the material shape of food into something beyond itself. But this transformation is more than just a material one – a change of shape. There is also a change in substance: the cook converts materiality into 'happiness'. Good household management goes beyond a clean and ordered household to a happy one. The matter that cleaning and ordering made ready for life, now goes out and lives.

Happiness is not something to be left to chance. Mrs Beeton follows with over 1,500 recipes, which are, in effect, short management plans for triumphing over 'the rude materialities of nature'. Even the most humble of these, such as No. 1132, 'Boiled Parsnips' (ibid.: 579), shows that dual process of reduction to order followed by surrounding with idealisms and graces that characterizes the management of civilization itself. By a series of actions the parsnips are progressively transformed: washing, scraping, removing specks, cutting, putting with boiling salted water, boiling until tender, draining, serving. At this point they intersect with the products of other transformations to form a dinner:

> Plan, Family Dinners for November . . . 2103. Wednesday. Boiled leg of pork, carrots, *parsnips*, and pease-pudding; fowl croquettes made with remainder of cold fowl. 2. Baroness pudding. (ibid.: 948, my italics)

It is in the act of consuming this dinner that a clean household becomes a happy and a civilized one. Its participants are taken up in a new order. It is an order that takes up and re-embodies its creators.

Mrs Beeton's management, however, as I remarked in Chapter 6, often has to be read against itself. Her myriad recipes can be a stimulus for a creative play with food that in turn stimulates the life for which the clean and orderly household stands ready. The results of all that cooking then re-embody the household as a place of civilization and happiness. These same recipes, however, can seem like another prescribed round of activity that anxiously fills the emptiness that has been cleared for it, not with celebration but with sheer weight and volume of complex products. Such a management fills time and space, but fails to make it live.

Compulsive Godliness

If the order that exceeds the body does not return and move that body, then it is not a meaningful organization, but merely an accumulation of objects and activities, neither alive nor animated. But the reverse is also true: if the only end of an order that exceeds the body is to stimulate the body, then excess becomes a compulsive seeking of sensation that vanishes as soon as it is experienced. The location of the result has merely been reversed. The body is only embodied in relation: it is not the origin and end of embodiment. This is apparent in the work of 'post-modern' management guru Tom Peters.

In Chapter 6, I noted Peters' complete reversal of the value of order, where no less than a wholesale embracing of chaos and disorder will restore life to the ailing, rule-bound enterprise. In some ways this advice is a rhetorical gesture aimed at alerting managers to that richness of life that, as Peters observes, seems 'abandoned at the front door of the business or public agency establishment' (1992: 375). So steeped is the management process in producing ordered and dominated spaces that only a mean and singular writing appears on its empty pages – Cixous' (Cixous and Clément, 1986: 95) 'thin thread, dry and taut'. Peters suggests an opening of the organization to the life that it has shut out. 'Why not think of fiction as a model for organization?' 'How about company-as-carnival?' (Peters, 1992: 15)

Peters is really in agreement with Mrs Beeton when he claims that good management is a process of moving beyond the materiality of existence:

'Matter is not all that matters'. (Stan Davis in *Future Perfect*) Value-added will come increasingly from intangibles, 'things' whose importance does not lie in their material existence. (Peters, 1992: 658)

It is fashion that represents 'the dominance of fickle, ephemeral software over solid hardware . . . Sure, there will be a 'hard' product (but) the significance of material goods (will be) as containers or vehicles for knowledge-value' (Peters, 1992: 7). Such precepts are not really so far removed from Mrs Beeton's 'triumphs over the rude materialities of nature'. It may come as no surprise to learn that she and her husband were also in the forefront of the fashion business, travelling to Paris to introduce the latest styles in affordable forms (Nown, 1986).

Management's preoccupation with the accumulation of results, Peters is suggesting, has no meaning if those results do not move us. To effectively manage, therefore, we must go beyond our own management, a paradox he acknowledges when he asks 'how do you *manage*, if that's the right word (and it's not), human imagination?' (Peters, 1992: 12). We have to both manage and not manage, Peters is suggesting, or manage, but not 'from the centre in a fickle economy' (Peters, 1992: 9). In this contradictory formulation Peters seems to be reaching towards a concept of the space of management very like Barthes' (1986: 59) 'paradoxical idea of structure: a system without end or center'.

However, there is something in Peters, as in Mrs Beeton, that also stills and fixes this paradoxical movement. If Mrs Beeton's sheer volume of recipes becomes an accumulation that eventually weighs down the imagination it was supposed to stimulate, Peters' similarly large volume of exhortation to embrace chaos exhausts through its unrelenting and frantic pace, where the assault on order and stability itself develops a sameness and predictability. Peters declares:

I'm fond of speaking of 'the four ephemerals': ephemeral organization . . . joined in ephemeral combinations . . . producing ephemeral products . . . for ephemeral markets . . . FAST. (Peters, 1992: 18)

Velocity, however, as Newton discovered, is only experienced when it changes. When there is no other speed than 'FAST', all speed is experienced as the same. The effect of Peters' hype over 763 pages is not so much argument as an unrelenting accumulation that swamps, and eventually wearies – this reader at least: I was never able to finish the book.

Where, for all Peters' talk of creativity, is the space for 'le silence habité des maisons'? For the 'reconciliation' of great art? Why is creativity only ever synonymous with 'frenzy', 'madness', 'flux', 'fickle', 'fashion'? As in Bergson, Peters' privileging of flux and change over fixity is tactical, but that tactic, pursued in a fixed manner, has a way of turning on itself as experience. As Game (1997: 3) puts it:

> In contemporary cultural theory, change, movement and multiplicity are valued as principles of meaning, knowledge and the self . . . There is a danger, however, that a simple privileging of movement and Heraclitean flux can end up reinventing what would be undone. Movement . . . can become curiously static.

Stasis is precisely the experience that Peters generates, a stasis that comes from an absence of relation – in this case the body's relation to what is outside it. We can see this more clearly by looking at Peters via Baudrillard. Peters' world of flux, fashion, and shifting desire is Baudrillard's (1983) 'hyperreality'. Hyperreality is a world of simulation, in which the simulacrum no longer refers back to a 'real'. There is no 'outside'. Starting from Borges' story about a map that is exactly the same extent and as detailed as the country it represents – a parody of representation – Baudrillard goes on to claim that the country itself has now vanished, and with it the meaning it gave to the map:

> Simulation is no longer that of a territory or a referential being or substance. It is the generation by models of a real without origin or reality: a hyperreal . . . it is no longer a question of either maps or territory. Something has disappeared; the sovereign difference that was the abstraction's charm. (Baudrillard, 1983: 2)

Hyperreality is premised on an *absence*, an absence of something beyond the imagination. It is the experience of that absence that generates the sense of unreality, and at the same time the anxiety to fill it. It is, I think, this anxiety that gives Peters' work that compulsive quality that is all too reminiscent of disembodying management.

Peters abandons the Taylorist project of the object world as the locus of control. There is no meaningful object world, only the ephemeral shiftings of desire. But when experience is only grounded in a subjectivity whose embodiment in the world of objects is forgotten, it becomes no more than a stream of sensations, an endlessly shifting spectacle that vanishes as soon as it is created. Experience becomes disembodied. Creativity, in a world whose materiality is simply 'forgotten', becomes a grab for attention, – whatever stands out for the moment from everything else and elicits 'Glow! Tingle! Wow! (Yuck!)' (Peters 1992: 663). Peters has an interesting anecdote about this:

> I paid full fare first class, about 800 or 900 smackeroos, for an American Airlines flight from Chicago to San Francisco. Yet on this four-hour, late-evening flight the crew couldn't even find a second bag of peanuts to serve. I was furious . . . Today, more than two years later, my 'no second bag of peanuts' memory is clear . . . We expect all long-distance calls to go through in a snap. We expect even a $7,000 car to start in 20-below-zero weather in Vermont. And we don't

expect the plane to crash! Our expectations about the raw, technical performance of almost everything are sky-high these days. So, fair or not, we take the hardest part for granted and focus on 'other'. (ibid.: 682–3)

Where life itself becomes the thrill produced by a second bag of peanuts, creativity and triviality become indistinguishable on the treadmill of new sensations. When the body loses its relation with its own order, it ceases to be experienced as body. It becomes a vacancy that demands to be filled, but like Borges' map in hyperreality, there will always be the lingering sense that it has filled nothing.

Metaphoric Play

Managing involves a relationship between our bodies and the outside world, a relationship that flows back and forth between them. This process I have characterized as metaphoric, but Terence Turner's (1991) account of how the Bororo people of Brazil manage the creation of an entire society shows not just one, but a number of metaphoric movements articulated together.

Turner centres his discussion around the claim of the Bororo people that they are, in fact, parrots, a claim that, as he says, 'after a century of anthropological exegesis (still) retains its frisson of irreducible alienness' (ibid.: 121). To make sense of the claim, Turner looks, not simply at the statement itself, but at the ritual managing of becoming parrots ('araras'). In examining the claim 'we are parrots' in action, he is led beyond a single metaphor explanation. He understands becoming parrots ('araras') as a 'play of tropes', or figures of speech, whose operation creates the ability 'to transcend the everyday social world and the power to encompass or subsume it as a whole within a 'higher' and more powerful totality' (ibid.: 140). In other words, it is, in Lefebvre's terms, about the creation of a new space of order.

A far-away order flows from the order of the body, and Bororo dancers prepare for the ceremony by adorning their bodies with the tail feathers of the arara. This, Turner claims, effects a metonymic association of the dancers with the araras: 'detached parts of real araras . . . now become parts of the new whole constituted by the dancer in his regalia' (ibid.: 147). In other words, the dancers re-embody a different order through a relation of contiguity with the birds. This re-creation of themselves, while involving metonymy as one trope, Turner points out, also involves metaphor as a second trope. The donning of the feathers implies the acquisition by the dancer of the arara powers of lightness and flight:

To become a flying being metaphorically means acquiring the power to separate oneself from one's normal terrestrial mode of social existence, in which one acts

within the received framework of social and cultural forms, and to assume an
external attitude toward that framework as a whole, a bird's eye view of it, as it
were. To don feathered regalia metaphorically figures the power to generate
form (in this case, social cultural form). (ibid.: 147)

There is an interesting parallel between the operation of externalizing
oneself described here, and that of making lists. Each involves a
metonymic re-ordering of the body through contiguity with something
outside it: araras, lists. But in both cases that re-ordering depends on a
metaphor: flying, time as space. This double movement, involving two
different tropes, re-embodies the participant as separated from and
external to the milieu in which they are immersed. When it is effective,
this movement is not disembodying. Rather it re-embodies the
participants as ordered more powerfully with respect to what is outside
them. For order to flow from the body it must first be embodied, and this
experience happens tropically.

This tropic re-embodiment creates a power that is, as yet, only potential.
The realization of that power, the creation of an outside order, Turner
contends, requires 'a third and higher level of tropic complexity' (ibid.:
148). The feathered dancers now move in patterns through the village
space, a movement that recreates that space itself as an arara. The metaphoric transformation of the attributes of araras, metonymically donned
with their feathered costumes, is now transferred to the village as a whole.
Turner identifies this as a movement of synecdoche, a trope whereby
the part becomes the whole, which in turn assumes the essential character
of its parts. The dance, he claims, effects a re-creation of social relations
that results in 'a dynamic synecdoche in which the ritual acts and
costumes become parts of a whole which they create in their own image'
(ibid.: 148).

The act of becoming araras, Turner contends, 'involves metonymy,
metaphor and synecdoche, in ascending order of complexity' (ibid.: 147).
Through this play of tropes, 'metaphor and its corollary tropic constructs
serve . . . as the central building blocks in the construction of a meaningful
world' (ibid.: 156). The play of tropes is an embodied process of organizing apparently disparate parts into new wholes, of creating new spaces
of meaning beyond 'the received framework of cultural forms'. It is a
syntax that, through the body, connects the different tropic movements
of metaphor, metonymy and synecdoche into an increasing level of
organization. It articulates its participants meaningfully in experience.

It is a feel for this sort of tropic movement as an organization and
development of experience that is, I think, more important than engaging
in some sort of intellectual game of 'name the trope'. In fact all these
tropes work metaphorically because they connect disparate terms through
embodied experience (dancers/feathers: metonymy; birds/power of
transcending the ordinary: metaphor; dancers/society: synecdoche).
Through this tropic movement the dancers embody a different sense of

order, which they then transfer to an outside. They, in turn, are taken up in this larger order that makes them more than what they were. On the face of it the claim that 'we are parrots' is a simple metaphor, but that metaphor conceals a complex exchange between the body and the outside world through a process that we can generally characterize as managing metaphorically.

Metaphoric Power

Turner describes the Bororo donning their feathered regalia as metaphorically figuring 'the *power* to generate form' (1991:147, my emphasis). The play of tropes is a *power*: a power to create order. But this power differs from that more usual characterization of power in management as bending nature, culture, and people to a preconceived intention. Ordione (1965: 39) puts this latter version unashamedly:

> The risk-oriented manager relates to his environment – including the people in it – in order to control it, to manipulate it, and to direct it for gain.

There is only a one-way movement here between the 'manager' and 'his environment', which is already thought of as 'his'. As an object it is set up, including the people in it, to be controlled, manipulated, and exploited for the benefit of a separated subject. As object, it does not participate in the creation of power. We have discussed this sort of power and the problems associated with it in Chapter 1.

Mary Parker Follett (1973: 72), writing in the early twentieth century, characterized this conception of power as 'power-over'. She was critical of this power because, in reducing people to no more than the function they occupied, it inevitably left a trace of resentment in that part of them that was excluded, a trace which, like friction in a machine, reduced the efficiency of the function being carried out. 'People do not like to be ordered, even to take a holiday' (ibid.: 32), Follett remarks.[2] Linstead (1993: 61) makes a similar observation via Canetti:

> Canetti (1962) defines power as the expression of order via command, command having two dimensions: *momentum* and *sting*. The momentum is the force upon the person to act, but the sting remains behind, invisible, indestructible and silent, perhaps for years, after every command is obeyed.

These accounts foreshadow Foucault's (1980) concept of power as relational, in the sense that where there is power there is always resistance. Because resistance is always present in power, Foucault argues, its work is never finished. There is always something that is a product of power, yet not absorbed into it. In fact, Bachelard (1983: 160) shows that resistance is necessary to experience power at all:

All constructive reveries – and there is nothing more essentially a builder than the reverie of power – are brought to life by the hope of surmounting adversity, by the vision of a vanquished adversary . . . It is pride that gives dynamic unity to a being; that is what creates and stretches the nerve fibres.

Victory in struggle against the elements, Bachelard claims, is the paradigm of this sort of constructive reverie. He recalls Nietszche's Zarathustra battling against the wind: 'walking is his battle. This it is what [sic] gives rhythmic energy to Zarathustra' (ibid.: 161). As an embodied experience, power is created by opposition; it follows, then, that the success of power destroys the experience. The body ceases to strain forward, the rhythmic energy dissipates. For the experience of power, resistance is something positive, and we saw in Chapter 1 how Taylor seemed to actively court resistance in order to experience struggle and feel alive. Yet for a management only interested in results, resistance can only be waste, and management has no use for waste. So management destroys what would give it life.

Follett's work is important for our purposes because she tries, in the context of management, to conceptualize a sense of power that does not dissipate with success. Follett had been a social worker, and was interested in the way a group seems to generate an energy that allows its members to solve problems they could not solve as individuals. Groups are spaces where individuals can exceed themselves. Here is a 'something over' that is not resistance, but excess. Groups, though she does not use the term, are a space of tropic transformation of the sort described by Turner. Recognizing this excess led Follett to propose a different conception of power, something that she called 'power-with':

> whereas power usually means power-over . . . it is possible to develop the conception of power-with, a jointly developed power, a co-active, not a coercive power. (1973: 72)

'Power-with' is a different conception of control, whose dynamic is not only realized through overcoming resistance. Follett specifically investigated the conditions under which orders did not automatically produce resistance – Canetti's 'sting'. To what, she asked, do we feel that we owe obedience? 'Surely only to a functional unity of which we are a part, to which we are contributing' (1973: 35). Such a 'functional unity' is more than a group of individuals, and more than a task. It is a 'situation' which everyone is involved in producing. Orders, Follett suggests, should flow from *situations*, not from *persons*. A personal order is, if effective, only a symbol that:

> we have both agreed, openly or tacitly, that that which I am ordering done is the best thing to be done. The order is then a symbol. (1973: 36)

An order, understood symbolically, is not automatically productive of resistance. The 'functional unity' that constitutes the situation, however, is not a static one where each participant's function is determined by a pre-existing whole, like the parts in a jigsaw. In a static unity the organization is self-identical. Even movement does not move. Here, for example, is an account of a situation where everything is in motion, and yet movement is blocked:

> Also it's a small town. People can't move in the same way, with people attracted to the organization or moving because they don't like it. So mobility's quite low. That's a contradiction because in the public service sense mobility's quite high. People always acting. It's just crazy for continuity or any sense of purpose. But in total terms I don't think anyone moves. It's just a lot of shaking.

Here is a space of motion which does not itself move. There is activity but no metaphoricity, no tropic play. The organization does not go forward: it vibrates or shakes. Movement that is not movement makes the organization hard to manage:

> It makes management difficult because one person can't be everything, and if you have some stability you learn that X will always get things done, or Y will have good ideas but talk forever, and so on, so you can put together a good decision. But that takes time, so it doesn't happen here. People aren't together for long enough.

While individual elements move, from the point of view of the whole, everything comes back to the same. The individual movements prevent that coming together of elements that would take them beyond themselves.

Follett reminds us that a dynamic unity is one where individuals experience involvement not just in their task, but in the whole as well:

> functional theory . . . tended to forget that our responsibility does not end with doing conscientiously and well our particular piece of the whole, but that we are also responsible for the whole. (1973: 51)

A relation, between the whole and its parts, that is created dynamically as a movement within a situation, means that managing, because it is that movement, can no longer be completely centralized. 'It should be recognized that almost everyone has some management ability,' Follett argues (1973: 57). This manager gives a sense of how management is diffused in this way in her organization:

> So the idea that let's have a teamwork approach so that no one individual has their strongly defined territory, to get people to respect each other's skills and start working together is about a process of working. That doesn't guarantee it's

going to work. But it's a way of working, a way of thinking that you take the risk that it's more likely to happen. You're never really sure about that . . . You can encourage and direct and nurture, create opportunities, but you can't control them so your level of influence – you don't really control it. You might like to, but you really don't. In the job I've had, I've had a lot of influence, but not control.

Power here is not synonymous with control, nor with the overcoming of resistance. Once people are taken beyond merely filling in as a particular piece of the whole, the whole itself changes. It becomes an energizing entity rather than something whose direction is already prescribed and circumscribed from outside. It becomes a relation between the body and the outside for everyone within it. There is still a manager, but that person is not a centre from which everything happens. Managing itself becomes more fluid, something that Denhardt (1981: ix–x) proposes:

> Leadership should not be seen merely as a position that someone holds, but rather as something that happens in a group or organization, something that comes and goes, something that ebbs and flows as the group or organization does its work . . . Anyone can be a leader, whether for a moment, for a few hours, a few days, a few weeks, or for years.

Metaphoric or tropic movement, however, is not a return to identity. 'X' does not remain 'X'. Managing may move beyond the manager. A willingness to create a vital organization is a generous impulse, a willingness to give away. For this manager, movement away from himself is a sign that things are going well:

> You know things are going well when you find out that something's happened that you didn't initiate. I mean it's within certain boundaries of what you're on about, but you had nothing to do with it. At [my previous workplace] that used to happen quite often, and it was great. That's the sort of organization I'd be wanting to try and achieve.

The organization, while still having a certain coherence, has a life in excess of and not dependent on him. Power does not emanate from and flow back to, a fixed point.

It would be a mistake, however, to reduce Follett's conception of 'power-with' to current preoccupations with teamwork. 'Power-with' flows from situations, not from persons, an insight that Follett herself does not rigorously pursue. She in fact recognizes this potential limitation in her work at the same time as she produces it by separating the 'psychological' from the 'technical':

> until we find some better way of uniting technical and so-called psychological problems than we have at present, we are far from efficient business administration. (1973: 61)

Perhaps because she does not succeed in uniting the 'psychological' and the 'technical', or because she insists on separating them, much of the potential influence of her work was sidelined into so-called personnel (later, human resources) management. Re-reading 'power-with' as a play of tropes by-passes this distinction because tropes cut across pre-given divisions between humanity and nature, psychology and technology.

As Whitehead pointed out, anything in the universe may be potentially related to anything else. So managing tropically, or metaphorically, is not just about managing people, it is a way of organizing through experience. Such organization is not just the manipulation of a tool or instrument by particular individuals or even groups to achieve particular ends, nor is it the sum of the struggles of those groups or individuals minus the resistance that these struggles generate. Organization may come about through the desire to achieve certain ends, but it is itself a more powerful way of being, that is really a continual becoming, and, as such, constantly transforms its ends. 'Power-with' cannot thus be shared, delegated or divided because it is just this capacity for becoming, as Follett was well aware:

> I do not think that power can be delegated because I believe that genuine power is capacity. (1973: 80)

Power, she understood, can be a generous overflowing of possibility rather than its coercion into the narrow channel of restraint.[3]

'A Sense of Moving Forward'

Let us now look at this power of tropic or metaphoric play in a situation of professional management. Here is one manager's account of what he finds satisfying in his job:

> to be able to, I suppose, pull together divergent strands or thoughts or concepts or groups, and be able to feed back to them what they are saying, but in a cohesive fashion. That they go 'Ah!' and there's a sense of moving forward, and those sorts of things. So it's about process to me, but process that leads to movement, to an organization actually picking itself up and moving along.

This manager understands order as movement, or, rather, a connection of movements – movements that flow between his body and a 'far-away'. All of these movements can be understood tropically. He first talks of a movement from outside toward himself, a 'pulling together'. This list of what he draws in is truly divergent: 'strands', 'thoughts', 'concepts', 'groups'. Here thought, people and material are not different categories of being, but all elements that go to make up a cohesive 'situation', in Follett's term. In an implicit metaphor of cooking, the separate ingredients are brought together by himself to embody a new whole in a process that can then 'feed back' to them. This process of nourishment is an organizing that creates wonder. People go 'Ah!' experiencing the organization anew. They come alive, and 'there's a sense of moving forward'. The process of taking in disparate elements and forming new wholes is that metaphoric ability assigned by Eliot to poets, but here directed to the organization of work.

He describes how he uses a planning process to get the organization moving beyond itself. His emphasis on movement leads him to reverse the usual priority of management, namely achieving particular ends:

> In many ways it doesn't actually matter what are the concrete things we're wanting to move on. I did a strategic planning process with the Centre that identified four new priorities. Now these priorities could have been any four.

On the face of it this seems a pretty alarming thing for a manager to be saying: that it does not really matter what the organization is doing. On reflection there are implied limits. The organizational context, a health centre, imposes a certain limitation on possible ends. It cannot become a butcher's shop, for example. Even within these implied limits, it is not suggested that any end is equivalent to any other, otherwise there would be nothing to argue about. The issue this manager is really raising is: what does the selection of particular ends actually mean? It seems to mean two things. First, priorities were selected. It is not that the achievement of particular ends is irrelevant. In fact a sense of movement is not possible without them, whether they are consciously articulated or not. Otherwise, as we saw in Chapter 5, we would simply be swept along in duration, in a flow of time. Movement itself, neither from anywhere or towards anywhere, would become an absolute, very like the fixity it supplanted.

What priorities also do is embody the organization outside itself, a movement that allows reflexivity:

> The whole organization sort of shaking itself out of its complacency – you know, 'we've always done these things so we'll keep doing them' – to take on that sense of reflection and self-challenge. To say what we are doing, or is this really working, or does this fit with where we want to be?

Priorities, like plans, may go wrong, fixing the organization in conformity with them, so that any future is merely an unravelling of the present, but they appear to work metaphorically in this case because they create movement, and a space for 'self-reflection and self-challenge'.

The initial movement in which this manager takes in diverse strands from outside and embodies them as a new whole is taken up by the organization in a movement of synecdoche, a movement analogous to the process whereby the feathered Bororo dancers, moving through the village, re-create it anew as their transformed selves. The planning process becomes a sort of dance that brings everybody in.[4] He now expresses the organization as doing what he seemed to be doing only as an individual at first. He moves from talking about 'I' and 'them' to 'we'. But because, through synecdoche, the whole assumes the essential character of its parts, then the parts also assume the character of the whole:

> And enough people in an organization actually start doing that. So rather than it just being me. But enough people are doing that so I can sit back and watch and see an organization get a sense of buzz and a sense of excitement about the work that it's doing, and to be able to argue with itself in a critical and progressive way on how it's working and where it's moving.

Successful managing creates a space of life and movement, 'a sense of buzz and a sense of excitement' that embodies the order it has produced. Here another manager speaks of that feeling in a way that seems very akin to the Bororo's feathered lightness:

> Oh, I feel light when things are going well, and when things aren't going well I feel heavy. The office feels lighter. The paperwork seems lighter. I probably walk with a lighter step.

That lightness, that sense that movement is easy, is not just a feeling of her own body, but of the whole environment that it is in as well. Herself, the office, and even the paper come together in a lightly moving unity, an experience of the metaphoric in action.[5] The buzz, lightness and effervescence of successful managing is an overflowing of power, but power in relation, not power-over.

Managing Well

Through managing well we create a body that is open to the possibilities of organizing beyond itself – a body that does not forget or kill itself through its order, but experiences itself and comes alive. We realize the metaphoricity of ourselves and of the outside world. Managing is a competence of living, as I have suggested in the introduction, but we can live well or badly through cleaning a piece of furniture or operating a business. If we manage well, the ordinary and the mundane, which we cannot avoid, become more than themselves: they live, and in that process we live through them. The results of managing well are not control and accumulation, but civilization. David Malouf (1980: 28) was aware of this when he wrote the following passage in *An Imaginary Life*. In it the poet Ovid, exiled to Asia Minor, contrasts the bleak landscape in which he can relate to nothing, to the Italy in which he properly lived:

> Do you think of Italy . . . as a place given to you by the gods, ready-made in all its placid beauty? It is not. It is a created place. If the gods are with you there, glowing out of a tree in some pasture or shaking their spirit over the pebbles of a brook in clear sunlight, in wells, in springs, in a stone that marks the edge

of your legal right over a hillside; if the gods are there, it is because you have discovered them there, drawn them up out of your soul's need for them and dreamed them into the landscape to make it shine. They are with you, sure enough. Embrace the tree trunk and feel the spirit flow back into you, feel the warmth of the stone enter your body, lower yourself into the spring as into some liquid place of your body's other life in sleep. But the spirits have to be recognized to become real. They are not outside us, or even entirely within, but flow back and forth between us and the objects we have made, the landscape we have shaped and move in. We have dreamed all these things in our deepest lives and they are ourselves. It is ourself we are making out there, and when the landscape is complete we shall have become the gods who are intended to fill it.

Nothing could better express that metaphoric ebb and flow between ourselves and the world that creates us as living relationally. If our managing achieves that, we have managed well.

Notes

1 I am not advocating management as a technique of self-development, because that would be merely shifting the location of the 'result', making the self the objective of managerial activity. Rather I am suggesting that management is embodied by its own processes whether it accepts or denies that. The order it achieves will affect it relationally, even if that relation is one of exclusion, Lefebvre's forgetting the body. The self will, therefore, necessarily be developed by the process of managing.

2 I had personal experience of this. One of my first acts as a manager was to review time-in-lieu, which involved telling the finance officer to take some of her accumulated time forthwith or she would risk losing it. I thought that by ordering her to take a holiday I was doing her a favour, but to my surprise this created considerable resentment because it completely disrupted the way she had planned to do her work.

3 It is such a power perhaps that Linstead (1996) has in mind when, following Deleuze and Guattari's (1984) body-without-organs, he celebrates the image of female ejaculation as an order that overflows the phallocentric strictures of modern organizations. It offers, he claims, something to replace:

> the now-defunct phallus as a sign to proceed under in our organizational deconstructions – joyous, inexhaustible, denied yet silenced for so long, a symbol of flows that flow from the body without organs, generous, transgressive, subversive, dissolving boundaries between binaries, refiguring our understandings of bodily control, and rewriting femininity.

4 I am reminded here of the title of Rosabeth Kanter's 'new management' text, *When Giants Learn to Dance* (1989). The new global economy, Kanter argues:

> requires more agile, limber management that pursues opportunity without being bogged down by the cumbersome structures or weighty procedures that impede action. Corporate elephants, in short, must learn how to dance. (20)

Unfortunately this rather whimsical prospect soon gets swept up in another project of mastery as Kanter assures US management that 'we can once again be masters, not victims of change'. Dancing then becomes no more than a limbering up for the global 'corporate Olympics' (ibid.: 19).

5 Durkheim (1965: 422) in fact describes the experience of the sacred in very similar terms, as a 'state of effervescence which changes the conditions of psychic activity'. In this state, he goes on to say, 'a man does not recognize himself; he feels transformed and consequently he transforms the environment which surrounds him.'

CONCLUSION: LETTING GO

By managing we create ourselves in relation to everything that is around us. We do not do this just as an intellectual exercise or an act of the will, but through the participation of our entire bodies in these relations. I have characterized this participation as metaphoric, because metaphor is just that enactment of the relational quality of the world through our embodied experience. It is the quality of the relations that we establish, or allow to establish themselves within us, that determines whether we have managed successfully or not.

Everybody is involved in managing, and it happens every day, but this is not to make it a trivial or a humdrum thing. It is in the everyday, now, when my body lives at this moment, that I experience triviality certainly, but it is equally when I experience pleasure, wonder, tragedy, pain, knowledge, civilization. The consequences of my managing may be inconsequential or momentous, but those consequences are happening now, for me, and that is true whether I am taking a bath, dining or drawing up next year's strategic plan. Professional management, I am then suggesting, should not be judged by any essentially different criteria to managing in the everyday: What is the quality of the relations it has established? How deeply does it embody us in living?

Professional management would be valued by its results. Fine, but how do we recognize a result when we see it? Because it conforms to something we predicted? But what sort of experience, we need to ask, is that, and why do we limit our notion of result to just that experience and not to others? Professional management, as I hope to have shown, too often cuts itself off from embodiment in living, the latter being relegated to mere process on the way to results – a means to an end, of no consequence in itself because any other means would do equally if the same end were to be reached. Management's achievements happen somehow outside that embodied living where managing happens. Having no body, they fail to satisfy, so yet more results must be pursued. We have visited at length the consequences of that outlook. Not surprisingly, professional management seems often impoverished and disorganized when compared to the managing that goes on outside or in spite of it.

Managing, I have argued, is metaphoric, and metaphor works through embodied experience. A management that is focused on the accumulation of results, that disembodies its own experience, cuts itself off from the richness and complexity of organizational possibility in which it is immersed. All around us, from the motions of the stars to the opening of plants and the coming and going of clouds, we can see forms of organization far more profound, delicate, robust and complex than anything depicted on an organizational chart, and requiring no human intervention whatever. Our own bodies are another case in point. The poverty of much of our sense of organization comes from an inability to participate in the organization that is all around and in us, and to allow and acknowledge its part in successful managing.

Managing flows from the situation and not just from the subject, be it the manager/subject, the organization/subject, or any central subject of control at all. Embodied managing is de-centred. Good managers, therefore, will pick up on and articulate possibilities of organization around them and encourage their development, but in no situation will a manager know entirely beforehand what these possibilities will be or how they will come about. Managing may require intervention, but it may equally require non-intervention; it may require clear direction, but it may also require a willingness to suspend or abandon direction; it may require vision, but it may equally require blindness, especially to its own vision.

The metaphoric character of managing means that to manage is not to achieve fixed ends, except as these are moments in a changing development of relations. This means that there is no point at which managing comes to a halt: its achievements are always relative. Experienced from an expectation of finality that flows from a desire to control, management can seem overwhelming and oppressive, like climbing a hill only to perceive a further hill beyond, and yet another beyond that. An unending achievement of goals vanishes as soon as it is achieved. Understanding that the relational character of experience is fundamental, and that its metaphoricity has no bounds, may help to situate the way boundaries and achievements can be either helpful stabilizers of experience, or frustrating illusions.

A related conclusion, if we take metaphoricity seriously as the basis of organization, is that managing only organizes through *undoing* itself. Organization does not accumulate in any quantitative way, as the project of a manageable world had hoped. This does not, however, mean abandoning order in a self-inflating embrace of chaos and ambiguity. Chaos and ambiguity embraced in this way simply become another fixity, the experience of which is already predetermined. Chaos and order, then, will always be drawing on one another, and threatening to undo one another also. Of course, at any given time the current emphasis in managing may alter. We may be holding on to a singular identity against perceived threats to its existence, or we may feel that a fixed identity is stagnating, and open it to the possibility of change. Once again, Simmel's image of the door is helpful: it may be experienced as closed or open at any particular time, but in either position it is still premised on a connection between two possibilities. Managing is about maintaining that relationship between order and disorder so we do not become fixed in the one or the other. To manage is to recognize the relational quality of experience. Control and order are not denied, but they are paradoxical.

The concept of managing that I have been exploring includes, but goes beyond, both the professional practice of management and the study of that practice. As an organizational principle in living it has implications for social and cultural theory in general. Metaphor works because the relational quality of the world can be experienced through our embodiment. Managing relates language, bodies, and the material world, and it can do so only because the boundaries between them are permeable. The activity of managing, therefore, challenges disciplinary boundaries that would separate the social–cultural from the natural, and the animate from the inanimate. To study managing is to rethink these disciplinary divisions, creating movement across their boundaries, a movement that is no more than evidence of continued vitality.

Leaving Management

I would prefer to end on a less abstract note as befits my theme of managing in experience. If managing is about developing a coherent yet changing organization, then it ultimately fails. Not only do all living organisms, including managers, eventually die, but as the second law of thermodynamics states, the energy in any system eventually dissipates, and the system runs down. Matter itself, it seems, eventually fails to manage. But, in a more limited sense, that metaphorical movement that links us to what is beyond ourselves can take us out of management, something that happened to me in the course of writing this book. I shall conclude with a brief account of how I experienced that, and how I managed it – an account that will show leaving management as another instance of my general theme.

Here is what I wrote in the couple of months before leaving my job:

> The place, the office, the organization, seems an irritating mess. No form or cohesion. Parts drifting off. Not peacefully, dissolving into something else, but incoherently. Today someone brought in a cake for morning tea. I didn't want to eat cake; I'm putting on weight. But I have a piece, and then a second that I really don't want.
>
> I feel invaded by work problems, but I don't know why. Yesterday, after a few drinks, I was overcome with anger at CT (one of our programme managers). It was over the introduction of a new performance appraisal system. She's very definite about having it, and seems to me over-controlling. I really couldn't care less about it, but I'm resisting one part of the organization being run differently from the rest. So I feel involved in a struggle of wills, which she probably sees as entirely negative, and which I don't really want. I'd rather not struggle, but if I let it go, what am I there for? So I assert my authority and say it has to be delayed until everyone's discussed it and it's approved by the Board. Yet this seems like a piece of pointless self assertion.

(Some days later)

I'm having a few days off in the country, but I wake up in the night thinking about the performance appraisal issue. I feel invaded, but I'm really struggling with myself. The house lightens with the dawn. Birds wake up, and only then can I drift off to sleep.

I should leave the place, but I seem to be waiting for some moment of coherence – something that will sum up the experience. I don't want to retreat in disorder, but nothing adds up. I can't imagine the whole enterprise coherently. My body doesn't feel coherent. I can't be in it or leave it behind.

Of course this is not naïve writing, uninfluenced by my thinking about management and organization, but neither was it written as a conscious illustration of my ideas. What I find interesting is the way neither myself nor the organization are organizing each other any more; but we are not indifferent to each other either. We are neither clearly engaged nor clearly disengaged. In the cake incident, I feel my body is getting out of control. I do not want to be nurtured by the place; it feels invasive, but I cannot prevent the invasion, and even multiply it. I want to deny the metaphoricity of a nurturing involvement with the organization, where it becomes me and I it, but paradoxically, I do this by accepting it in a way that is not metaphorical. I take in the cake, but it remains not me, contributing to a body I do not want to be part of.

The conflict over performance appraisal leads me to no sense of movement, but it does not leave me still either. It simply makes me assert my role as manager, trying to maintain a coherence I do not experience. Managing, then, becomes just a role, and one I resent having to do. I am immersed in a self and a body I do not want, even when I try to escape from it on holiday. I finally escape into sleep as the house 'lightens' with the dawn, and I 'lighten' metaphorically, temporarily flowing out of myself as the outside flows into me. Here, at last, is a reciprocal movement that works; in all this muddle, a moment of managing.

Interestingly, I know I should leave, but I am waiting for a moment of coherence, of significance, of summing up: a moment that signifies a definite break. We are used to thinking of ending in this way, as a boundary, or a point in time, but it is actually the *experiencing* of such a boundary or point that creates the coherence of an end. Without it, there is only that nebulous and polluting ambiguity that Mary Douglas (1966) speaks of – an inability to separate ourselves from the rubbish. Ending, in duration, is often a muddle. We think it is ourselves who are leaving, but it is our work, too, that is leaving us. Recalling Calvino's story of putting out the rubbish, we are that rubbish. This means, of course, that the actual act of leaving does not necessarily resolve the muddle. We take the rubbish with us. To experience an end, we have to re-create ourselves in relation to that rubbish.

This became apparent when I had finally left my management position to complete this writing. To manage leaving, an end had to be created. Here is a note I made a couple of weeks after leaving:

I rang work, rather reluctantly, to return a call from BC. She sounded quite distant. She made it quite clear that she was ringing on a work matter, and only 'because R had told me to'. I tried to make small talk, but she politely refused. I felt irked by this for some time. Guilty for having left them in funding uncertainty. Annoyed that she made me feel guilty. Or was I imagining it? I fantasized about situations where she would approach me and I would cut off her friendliness with cool politeness. When I'm made to feel the bad guy, I want to attack.

I do not want to contact work, but when I do, I want everyone to like me. That would make a happy ending. But really it is myself that I am not liking. Although wanting to stay distant, I do not want to be put at a distance, because it reminds me that I am not, in fact, distant, but still there in a way I do not want to be. So I fantasize about being able to create distance, displaying a power I do not have.

I received a lot of goodbye cards, but at this stage I had not actually read any of them. I also experienced an extreme reluctance to write about what I was experiencing, although I felt I should keep a diary of it as part of my book work. Writing about it seemed to be trivial, and wasting time that I should be spending on 'real' studying and writing. I also had a sense that if I started writing this diary, it could be unlimited, with no evident boundaries, and so endlessly intrude on time I regarded as precious. The experience of leaving was still, in Mary Douglas' phrase, 'matter out of place', but also matter out of time. It was present, but I could find no time for it.

As it happened, keeping that experience and this book apart was not so easy. One of our branches had organized a farewell dinner for me. I was very reluctant to go, 'forgetting' about the occasion at least twice. The day before the dinner, I sat down to write as usual, but could do nothing. I just stared at the blank page, which seemed more like a wall than an invitation. I took my car off to be serviced. The garage was several kilometres away, and I decided to walk back home via the beach. It was a beautiful day, and the seas were very big. Instead of going directly home, I went around to look at the ocean from some rocks directly below a flat where I used to live. I realized that, though I still lived nearby, I had not come to this place for a long time. Work schedules did not seem to allow time for just sitting and looking. As I sat, absorbed in that movement 'inhuman, of the veritable ocean', I started thinking about what was good and bad in my experience as manager, and I realised I was composing a farewell speech, in case one was needed at the dinner. I did not want just a superficial speech, but to acknowledge what I owed to the organization, and my disengagement and dissatisfaction as well: in the words of a rather more famous farewell speech, to 'nothing extenuate, nor set down ought in malice'.

As I sat thinking and watching the big waves sweep past, I noticed something I had never seen before. As a wave came near the shore and started breaking, it would curl over, and the foam would start racing down the slope of the wave itself, sparkling as it was driven along. It was as though the wave were surfing on itself. It was a frolicsome, delightful movement, and I watched it for a long time, utterly rapt. It made me feel that I, too, could go ahead of myself, of my past, playing beyond what I had accumulated, but only on the basis of that. I felt too, being back in an old place, one that was part of me before this job, that I had a past, but also that I was still here. Just as we saw, in Chapter 6, that a new beginning could not be entirely empty or there would be nothing to begin, so an ending cannot be entirely empty either. For it to be experienced as an end, something must continue beyond it, and that something must be made from what has been left behind. Endings and beginnings are thus related.

I went home and wrote out the speech and went to the dinner with a better grace. A speech was needed, but something less formal than what I had composed. So I gave one, based on what I had written, but I felt it was inadequate. Spontaneity actually makes me anxious, and I would have preferred something more 'finished'. But it sufficed, and so with the help of the ocean, the past, my colleagues and friends, I had begun to manage my way out of management, if not out of managing.

REFERENCES

Abrams, M. H. (1953) *The Mirror and the Lamp*. Oxford: Oxford University Press.

Alvesson, M. (1993) 'The Play of Metaphors', in Hassard, J. and Parker, M. eds *Postmodernism and Organizations*. London: Sage.

Alvesson, M. and Willmott, H. eds (1992) *Critical Management Studies*. London: Sage.

AS/NZS ISO 9000–9004 (1994) *Quality Management and Quality Assurance Standards*. Homebush: Standards Australia/ Standards New Zealand.

Auer, J., Repin, Y., and Roe, M. (1993) *Just Change: The Cost-Conscious Manager's Toolkit*. Wollongong: National Reference Centre for Primary Health Care.

Bachelard, G. (1969) *The Poetics of Space*. tr. M. Jolas. Boston: Beacon Press.

Bachelard, G. (1983/1949) *Water and Dreams*. tr. E. Farrell, Dallas: The Pegasus Foundation.

Barthes, R. (1986) *The Rustle of Language*. tr. R. Howard, Oxford: Blackwell.

Baudrillard, J. (1983) *Simulations*. tr. P. Foss, P. Patton and P. Beitchman, New York: Semiotext(e) Inc.

Beeton, Mrs. I. (1861, facsimile 1968) *The Book of Household Management*. London: Jonathan Cape.

Bergson, H. (1950/1910) *Time and Free Will*. tr. F.L. Pogson, London: George Allen and Unwin.

Bird, C. (1994) *Not Now Jack – I'm Writing a Novel*. Sydney: Picador.

Black, M. (1962) *Models and Metaphors*. Ithaca: Cornell University Press.

Boje, D., Gephart, R., and Tojo, J. eds (1996) *Postmodernism and Postmodern Organization Theory*. Thousand Oaks: Sage.

Braverman, H. (1974) *Labor and Monopoly Capital*. New York and London: Monthly Review Press.

Burrell, G. (1992) 'The Organization of Pleasure', in Alvesson, M. and Willmott, H. eds *Critical Management Studies*. London: Sage.

Burrell, G. and Morgan, G. (1978) *Sociological Paradigms and Organizational Analysis*. London: Heinemann.

Byatt, A.S. (1993) 'Art Work', *The Matisse Stories*, London: Chatto and Windus.

Caesar, J. (1967) *The Civil War*. tr. J. Mitchell, Harmondsworth: Penguin Books.

Calvino, I. (1993) 'La Poubelle Agréée', in *The Road to San Giovanni*. tr. T. Parks, Jonathan Cape.

Chandler, A.D. (1962) *Strategy and Structure: Chapters in the History of the American Industrial Enterprise*. Cambridge, Mass.: MIT Press.

Chia, R. (1996) *Organizational Analysis: a Deconstructive Approach*. Berlin and New York: Walter de Gruyter.

Cixous, H. and Clément, C. (1986/1975) *The Newly Born Woman*. tr. B. Wing, Minneapolis: University of Minnesota Press.

Clawson, D. (1980) *Bureaucracy and the Labor Process*. New York and London: Monthly Review Press.

Clegg, S. (1990) *Modern Organizations*. London and Newbury Park: Sage.

Clegg, S. (1992) 'Postmodern Management?', *Journal of Organizational Change Management*, 5(2): 31–49.

Collinson, D.L. and Hearn, J. eds (1996) *Men as Managers, Managers as Men*. London: Sage.

Copley, F.B. (1969/1923) *Frederick W. Taylor, Father of Scientific Management*. (2 vols) Augustus M. Kelly.

De Certeau, M. (1988) *The Practice of Everyday Life*. tr. S. Rendall, Berkeley: University of California Press.

Deetz, S. (1992) *Democracy in an Age of Corporate Colonization*. Albany: State University of New York Free Press.

Deleuze, G. and Guattari, F. (1984) *Anti-Oedipus: Capitalism and Schizophrenia*. London: Athlone Press.

Denhardt, R.B. (1981) *In the Shadow of Organization*. Kansas: University Press of Kansas.

Derrida, J. (1976) *Of Grammatology*. tr. G. C. Spivak, Baltimore and London: The Johns Hopkins University Press.

Derrida, J. (1982) *Margins of Philosophy*. tr. A. Bass, Brighton: Harvester Press.

Descartes, R. (1985) *Rules for the Direction of the Mind*. tr. J. Cottingham, R. Stoothoff, and D. Murdoch, Cambridge: Cambridge University Press.

Douglas, M. (1966) *Purity and Danger*. London and Henley: Routledge and Kegan Paul.

Drucker, P. (1954) *The Practice of Management*. New York and Evanston: Harper and Row.

Durkheim, E. (1965/1915) *The Elementary Forms of Religous Life*. tr. J. Swain, New York: The Free Press.

Edwards, R. (1979) *Contested Terrain. The Transformation of the Workplace in the Twentieth Century*. London: Heinemann.

Eliot, T. S. (1963) 'The Metaphysical Poets (1921)', *Selected Essays*. London: Faber and Faber.

Engels, F. (1958/1876) 'The Part Played by Labour in the Transition from Ape to Man', in Marx, K. and Engels, F. *Selected Works Vol. II*. tr. Institute of Marxism-Leninism. Moscow: Foreign Languages Publishing House.

Follett, Mary Parker (1973) *Dynamic Administration*. Collected Papers, ed. E.M. Fox and L. Urwick, Belmont: Pitman Publishing.

Foucault, M. (1970) *The Order of Things*. London: Tavistock.

Foucault, M. (1973) *The Birth of the Clinic*. tr. A.M. Sheridan Smith, London: Tavistock Publications.

Foucault, M. (1980a) *Power/Knowledge*. ed. C. Gordon, Sussex: The Harvester Press.

Foucault, M. (1980b) *The History of Sexuality, Volume One. An Introduction*. tr. R. Hurley, Harmondsworth: Penguin.

Foucault, M. (1991) *Discipline and Punish*. tr. A. Sheridan, Harmondsworth: Penguin Books.

Freud, S. (1984) 'Mourning and Melancholia', *On Metapsychology: The Theory of Psychoanalysis*. Vol. XI, The Pelican Freud Library, Ringwood: Penguin.

Fry, J. ed. (1986) *Toward a Democratic Rationality*. Aldershot: Gower.

Gallop, J. (1988) *Thinking through the Body*. New York: Columbia University Press.

Game A. (1991) *Undoing the Social*. Milton Keynes: Open University Press.

Game, A. (1994) 'Matter Out of Place: The Management of Academic Work', *Organization*, 1(1): 47–50.

Game, A. (1997) 'Time Unhinged'. *Time and Society*, 6(2/3): 115–29.

Game, A. and Metcalfe, A. (1996) *Passionate Sociology*. London: Sage.

Gergen, K.J. (1992) 'Organization Theory in the Postmodern Era', in Reed, M. and Hughes, M. eds *Rethinking Organization*. London: Sage.

Gouldner, A.W. (1969) 'The Unemployed Self', in Fraser, R. ed. *Work, Vol II*. Harmondsworth: Penguin Books.

Gowler, D. and Legge, K. (1983) 'The Meaning of Management and the Management of Meaning: a View from Social Anthropology', in Earl, M.J. ed. *Perspectives on Management*. Oxford University Press.

Gurvitch, G. (1990) 'The Problem of Time', in Hassard, J. ed. *The Sociology of Time*. New York: St Martins Press.

Hamel, G. and Prahalad, C.K. (1989) 'Strategic Intent', *Harvard Business Review*, May–June: 63–76.

Hammer, M. and Champy, J. (1993) *Re-engineering the Corporation: A Manifesto for Business Revolution*. London: Nicholas Brealy.

Hassard, J. (1996) 'Exploring the Terrain of Modernism and Postmodernism in Organization Theory', in Boje, D., Gephart, R., and Tojo, J. eds *Postmodernism and Postmodern Organization Theory*. Thousand Oaks: Sage.

Hassard, J. and Parker, M. (1993) *Postmodernism and Organizations*. London: Sage.

Hawe, P., Degling, D., and Hall, J. (1990) *Evaluating Health Promotion: A Health Worker's Guide*. Sydney: MacLennan and Petty.

Hayles, C.P. (1986) 'What Do Managers Do? A Critical Review of the Evidence', *Journal of Management Studies*, 23(1): 88–115.

Hearn, J., Sheppard, D., Tancred-Sheriff, P., and Burrell, G. eds (1989) *The Sexuality of Organization*. London: Sage.

Heidegger, M. (1977) *The Question Concerning Technology and other Essays*. tr. W. Lovitt, New York and London: Garland Publishing Inc.

Jackall, R. (1988) *Moral Mazes: The World of Corporate Managers*. Oxford: Oxford University Press.

Kakar, S. (1970) *Frederick Taylor: A Study in Personality and Innovation*. Cambridge, Mass.: The MIT Press.

Kanter, R.M. (1977) *Men and Women of the Corporation*. New York: Basic Books.

Kanter, R.M. (1989) *When Giants Learn to Dance*. London: Simon and Schuster.

Karpin Report (1995) Industry Task Force on Leadership and Management Skills, *Enterprising Nation*. Canberra: Australian Government Publishing Service.

Kerfoot, D. and Knights, D. (1996) '"The Best is Yet to Come?": The Quest for Embodiment in Managerial Work', in Collinson, D.L. and Hearn, J. eds *Men as Managers, Managers as Men*. London: Sage.

Knights, D. and Willmott, H. eds (1986) *Managing the Labour Process*. Aldershot: Gower.

Koontz, H. and O'Donnell, C. (1978) *Essentials of Management*. New York: McGraw-Hill.

Lakoff, G. and Johnson, M. (1980) *Metaphors We Live By*. Chicago: University of Chicago Press.

Lawrence, D.H. (1960) *Psychoanalysis and the Unconscious and Fantasia of the Unconscious*. New York: Viking Press.

Lawrence, D.H. (1961) *Selected Literary Criticism*. ed. A. Beal. London: Mercury Books.

Lawson, J.S. (1992) *Planning, Organising and Managing Modern Hospitals and Health Services – An Introduction*. Sydney: School of Health Services Management, The University of New South Wales.

Leavis, F.R. (1963) 'Literary Criticism and Philosophy', *The Common Pursuit*. Harmondsworth: Penguin Books.

Le Doeuff, M. (1989) *The Philosophical Imaginary*. tr. C. Gordon, Stanford: Stanford University Press.

Lefebvre, H. (1991) *The Production of Space*. tr. D. Nicholson-Smith. Oxford, UK and Cambridge, Mass.: Blackwell.

Linstead, S. (1993) 'Deconstruction in the Study of Organizations', in Hassard, J. and Parker, M. eds *Postmodernism and Organizations*. London: Sage.

Linstead, S. (1996) 'The Control of Fluidity and the Fluidity of Control: Towards the Organization-without-Organs?' Paper presented to 'The Body and Organization' Conference, Keele University, Staffordshire, UK, September 1996.

Littler, C.R. (1982) *The Development of the Labour Process in Capitalist Societies*. London: Heinemann Educational Books.

Lobel, A. (1992) *Frog and Toad Together*. London: Mammoth.

Loy, D. (1988) *Nonduality*. Newhaven and London: Yale University Press.

Loy, D. (1992) 'Avoiding the Void: The Lack of Self in Psychotherapy and Buddhism', *The Journal of Transpersonal Psychology*, 24(2): 151–79.

Macken, D. (1997) 'How Did We Ever Manage', *Good Weekend*, April 5: 46.

Malouf, D. (1980) *An Imaginary Life*. Sydney: Picador.

Marshall, J. and Stewart, R. (1981) 'Managers' Job Perceptions, II', *Journal of Management Studies*, 18(3): 263–75.

Marx K. (1958/1888) 'Theses on Feuerbach', in Marx, K. and Engels, F. *Selected Works Vol. II*. tr. Institute of Marxism-Leninism. Moscow: Foreign Languages Publishing House.

Merleau-Ponty, M. (1964) *The Primacy of Perception*. ed. J.M. Edie, Evanston: Northwestern University Press.

Merleau-Ponty, M. (1968) *The Visible and the Invisible*. tr. A. Lingis, Evanston: Northwestern University Press.

Merleau-Ponty, M. (1974) 'The Philosopher and Sociology', in O'Neill, J. ed. *Phenomenology, Language and Sociology*. London: Heinemann.

Metcalfe, A.W. (1995) 'The Hands of Homo Faber', *Body and Society*, 1(2):105–126.

Metzner, R. (1994) 'Addiction and Transcendence as Altered States of Consciousness', *Journal of Transpersonal Psychology*, 26(1): 1–17.

Mintzberg, H. (1973) *The Nature of Managerial Work*. New York: Harper and Row.

Morgan, G. (1980) 'Paradigms, Metaphors and Puzzle Solving in Organizational Theory', *Administrative Science Quarterly*, 25(4): 605–22.

Morgan, G. (1983) 'More on Metaphor: Why We Cannot Control Tropes in Administrative Science', *Administrative Science Quarterly*, 28(December): 601–7.

Morgan, G. (1986) *Images of Organization*. Beverly Hills: Sage.

Murrell, K.F.H. (1965) *Ergonomics: Man in His Working Environment*. London: Chapman and Hall.

Nown, G. (1986) *Mrs Beeton: 150 Years of Cookery and Household Management*. London: Ward Lock Limited.

Offre, C. (1976) *Industry and Inequality*. London: Arnold.

Ordione, G. (1965) *Management by Objectives*. Belmont: Pitman Publishing Corporation.

Parker, M. (1992) 'Post-Modern Organizations or Postmodern Organization Theory?', *Organization Studies*, 13(1): 1–17.

Parker, M. (1993) 'Life After Jean-François', in Hassard, J. and Parker, M. eds *Postmodernism and Organizations*. London: Sage.

Patterson, J. (1993) 'Beyond Case Payments: a new paradigm for Australian health and welfare', in Economic Planning and Advisory Council, *Investing in Health: A Challenging Future*. Canberra: Australian Government Publishing Service.

Peters, T. (1987) *Thriving on Chaos*. London: Macmillan.

Peters, T. (1992) *Liberation Management*. London: Macmillan.

Pollitt, C. (1993) *Managerialism and the Public Services*. Oxford: Blackwell.

Pringle, R. (1988) *Secretaries Talk*. Sydney: Allen and Unwin.

Reed, M. (1989) *The Sociology of Management*. London: Harvester Wheatsheaf.

Reed, M. (1990) 'From Paradigms to Images: The Paradigm Warrior turns Post-Modernist Guru', *Personnel Review*, 19(3): 35–40.

Reed, M. and Hughes, M. (1992) *Rethinking Organization*. London: Sage.

Rees, S. and Rodley, G. (1996) *The Human Costs of Managerialism*. Leichhardt: Pluto Press Australia.

Richards, I.A. (1936) *The Philosophy of Rhetoric*. Oxford: Oxford University Press.

Richardson, J. (1986) *Wallace Stevens: The Early Years 1879–1923*. New York: Beech Tree Books, William Morrow.

Ricoeur, P. (1977) *The Rule of Metaphor*. London and Henley: Routledge and Kegan Paul.

Salaman, G. (1981) *Class and the Corporation*. Glasgow: Fontana.

Sheldrake, R. (1989) *The Presence of the Past*. Glasgow: Fontana.

Simmel, G. (1994) 'Bridge and Door', *Theory, Culture and Society*, 11(1): 5–10.

Spain, N. (1948) *Mrs Beeton and Her Husband*. London: Collins.

Spriegel, W. and Myers, C. eds (1953) *The Writings of the Gilbreths*. Illinois: Richard D. Irwin.

Stewart, R. (1967) *The Reality of Management*. London: Pan.

Stewart, R. (1983) 'Managerial Behaviour: How Research has Changed the Picture', in Earl, M.J. ed. *Perspectives on Management*. Oxford University Press.

Stryk, L. and Ikemoto, T. ed. and tr. (1981) *The Penguin Book of Zen Poetry*. Harmondsworth: Penguin Books.

Suzuki, D.T. (1927) *Essays in Zen Buddhism*. London: Luzac and Co.

Taylor, F. (1911) *The Principles of Scientific Management*. NY and London: Harper and Bros.

Thomas, T.T. (1977) *100 Walks in New South Wales*. Melbourne: Hill of Content.

Tsoukas H. (1993) 'Analogical Reasoning and Knowledge Generation in Organization Theory', *Organization Studies*, 14(3): 323–46.

Turner, B.S. (1984) *The Body and Society*. Oxford: Basil Blackwell.

Turner T. (1991) '"We are Parrots, Twins are Birds": Play of Tropes as Operational Structure', in Fernandez, J.W. ed. *Beyond Metaphor*. Stanford: Stanford University Press.

Varela, F.J., Thompson, E., and Rosch, E. (1991) *The Embodied Mind*. Cambridge, Mass. and London: MIT Press.

Wastewater Source Control Branch (1994) *Information Kit*. Sydney: Water Board.

Weber, M. (1949) *The Methodology of the Social Sciences*. tr. and ed. E.A. Shils and H.A. Fuch, NY: The Free Press.

Wensley, R. (1996) 'Isabella Beeton: Management as "Everything in its Place"', *London Business School Business Strategy Review*, 7(1): 37–46.

Whitehead, A.N. (1978/1929) *Process and Reality*. Corrected Edition ed. D.R. Griffin and D.W. Sherburne, NY: The Free Press.

Williams, R. (1983) *Keywords*. London: Flamingo.

Wordsworth, W. (1800) 'Preface to the Second Edition of Lyrical Ballads, 1800', in Jones, E. ed., (1940) *English Critical Essays: Nineteenth Century*, London: Oxford University Press.

Wynne, B. (1987) *Risk Management and Hazardous Waste*. Berlin: Springer Verlag.

Yeatman, A. (1987) 'The Concept of Public Management and the Australian State in the 1980s', *Australian Journal of Public Administration*, 46(4): 339–56.

Yeatman, A. (1990) *Bureaucrats, Technocrats, Femocrats*. Sydney: Allen and Unwin.

Zinchenko, V. and Munipov, V. (1989) *Fundamentals of Ergonomics*. tr. I. Kochiley, Moscow: Progress Publishers.

INDEX

Bold page numbers indicate a main entry in the text